CW00706381

Discovering Th

Discovering
The Pennines

RON & MARLENE FREETHY

JOHN DONALD PUBLISHERS LTD
EDINBURGH

ISBN 0 85976 359 5

British Library Cataloguing in Publication Data
A catalogue record for this book is available from
the British Library.

Phototypeset by The Midlands Book Typesetting Company,
Loughborough.
Printed & bound in Great Britain by J. W. Arrowsmith Ltd., Bristol.

Introduction

When we were first asked by the Publishers to add this title to their expanding number of titles in the *Discovery* series we were, for once, reluctant even though we knew the area well. We already had a goodly collection of walking books on *The Pennine Way* and adding one more did not seem a good idea. Our editor pointed out that what was wanted was not a route march along the backbone of England but a description of towns and villages which would provide the explorer with a historical, geographical and accommodation focus from which a series of short walks could be made. We had one further tongue-in-cheek reservation — why should we write a book about a fraud? In 1747 Charles Bertram forged a Roman History of Britain which he called *On the State of Britain* and in which he referred to the hills running through the North of England as the 'Alpes Penina'. Looking back so far into history it is difficult to be sure whether Bertram was a crook or whether he merely had a wicked sense of humour. In any event the forgery was rumbled but for ever after the name stuck and 'The Pennines' were duly named. We have been able to link together several areas including the Derbyshire Peak, a flirtation with Cheshire, the South West Pennines of Industrial Yorkshire and Lancashire, the Yorkshire Dales, parts of Cumbria, Durham, Northumberland and beyond these to the Cheviot Hills and the borders of Scotland to produce a unified whole. At last we had a true perspective of the Pennines — a blend of geology, history and natural history and therefore a suitable companion to the other volumes we have contributed to the series.

We are grateful to a number of friends for the use of their photographs including Bob Smithies, Bill Wilkinson and Alex Tewnion who provided the picture of the arctic hare. We also extend our thanks to the staff of all the Information Centres who so willingly helped us.

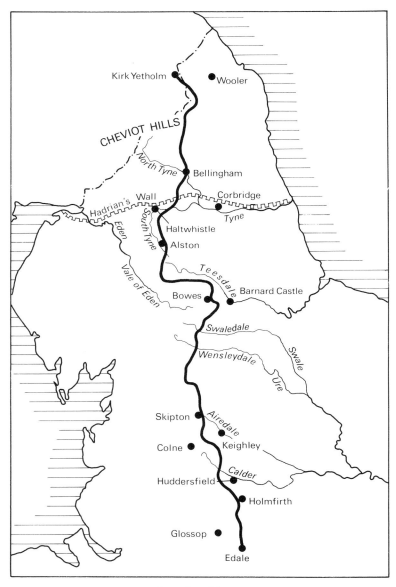

Location Map

Contents

CHAPTER 1

A Pennine Portrait

The Pennines are the backbone of Northern England and take no account whatever of county boundaries but why indeed should they? County boundaries are subject to changes once as a result of wars, but now because of political pressures. The Pennines themselves are literally as old as the hills and it is only in popular songs that faith can move mountains.

The Pennines are basically a range of hills and mountains running in a mainly north south direction from the Tyne Gap to the Midland Plain. The range is generally monoclinal in the north and tilted slightly towards the east with many faults on the western side. To south of the Aire Gap the Pennines become more anticlinal and this means far fewer sharp escarpments and thus produces a more rounded appearance. In some sense the Pennines and the Pennine Way differ, the latter being a long distance footpath of 256 miles which has been extended beyond the physical limits of the Pennines to take the walker through into Kirk Yetholm which is just in Scotland via the Cheviots. We decided to allow ourselves the luxury of including this last section in the present book partly because it is neater and more complete when covered in this way, but most of all because we love the country.

The Pennine range fascinates geologists because within it are two of the most important limestone areas in Britain, around the Derbyshire Peak and the Craven Dales in Yorkshire.

Like any upland area the Pennines are subject to high rainfall and regular heavy snow in winter. This can cause chaos to cross-Pennine traffic and the Snake Pass between Manchester and Sheffield, the M62 motorway and the A66 between Penrith and Scotch Corner through Teesdale are always among the first to close. Wherever there is rain and snow-melt spating rivers are produced and the erosion of contrasting rocks produce some of Britain's most exciting waterfalls including Cauldron Snout and High Force in Teesdale, Aysgarth, Cotter Force and Hardraw in the Yorkshire Dales, Ingleton and Scaleber Force in the Craven Dales plus other smaller but impressive falls in the Derbyshire hills.

The idea of considering the Pennines as a whole was only brought into sharp focus when the long distance footpath was being planned from around 1951 prior to the much publicised opening on 24 April 1965. On 22 June 1985 the Pennine Way Council met on Malham Moor to celebrate the initial idea of the footpath which was pioneered by the veteran walker Tom Stephenson in 1935. Perhaps the project would have taken shape much sooner had it not been for the advent of the Second World War. Tom Stephenson died in 1987 in his 95th year — what an advert for a lifetime of strenuous walking!

The Pennines at either end rise to around 2000 feet (609.3 metres) and therefore qualify as genuine mountains but on the 35 mile stretch around the Aire Gap few peaks exceed half this figure. The narrowest area is sandwiched between Rochdale in Lancashire and Huddersfield in Yorkshire. To the north of the Aire Gap the peaks suddenly increase in height and dramatic effect with the most easterly of these mountains being the magnificent Great Whernside which is the watershed of the River Nidd. At Stainmore the Pennines narrow once more and here is the highest point of the whole range on the plateau summit of Cross Fell which is 2,930 feet (897 metres) above sea-level.

The Key to the wildlife of any area is the underlying rocks and the broad uplift which we know generally as the Pennines is often of Carboniferous material laid down when the area was covered by a shallow tropical sea around 265 million years ago. At the south of the range is the Peak District, which many describe as limestone, whereas in fact there is a relatively small area of exposed limestone ringed by gritstone. The limestone was formed as the bodies of marine organisms with skeletons of calcium carbonate were compressed over thousands of years by other shells sinking down upon them. As the seas evaporated they were still fed by mighty rivers and the debris brought down by these created deltas of gritstone. In the southern Pennines there is just a little uncovered limestone, but lots of gritstone once used to make millstones and hence became known as millstone grit, plus an extensive area of coal measures. The latter were formed by huge plants related to ferns growing in the damp warm climate and their remains being crushed by more heavy vegetation growing, dying and falling on the debris. The varying speed of erosion of different areas has produced the scenery we find today and also determined the industry be it mining for coal or minerals or quarrying for limestone or millstone grit.

Much of the Yorkshire Dales consists of exposed areas of limestone which are referred to as the Yoredale series because they were first studied in the valley of the River Yore which was later named the Ure. Because the River Ure flows through the village of Wensley which, until devastated by the Black Death, had an important market the area has become known as Wensleydale. Typical of Wensleydale is what has been described as Step-Topography caused by the fact that the different layers of rock have eroded at different rates producing not only dramatic waterfalls, but also hillsides which do resemble wide ladder like ridges although on a huge scale and which often provide havens for increasingly rare plants easily destroyed by careless human footsteps. In geological terms this area is not very complicated and is based upon two zones, the Askrigg block composed of limestone around the town of the same name in Wensleydale and the Alston block which is a huge slab of granite around the north Cumbrian town. Any differences in the scenery is due to the different rocks and the erosion caused by centuries of different weather patterns prevailing around the two areas.

In contrast the geology of the Howgill Fells which lies between the two is more complex and best viewed from the M6 motorway which punches its way along the Lune Valley. There are some spectacular views from the south-bound service station overlooking Killington reservoir. For those who wish to explore the area at leisure then the Sedbergh to Tebay road is an ideal route with a diversion from the Cross Keys Inn, now a National Trust cafe serving excellent ham and eggs, to the dramatic Cautley Spout as it tumbles over the dark crag.

Beyond Penrith is Alston standing on a block of volcanic granite and at the head of the valley of the South Tyne and thus stands at the end of the Pennine chain proper. The main street of Alston has a gradient of 1 in 10 and at more than 1000 feet (305 metres) is said to be Britain's highest market

Alston — A typical Pennine town.

town. The A686 road from Penrith is the highest A road in England reaching an altitude of 1903 feet (580 metres). The Eden is virtually the boundary river in this area and the edge of the Pennine range is known locally as the East Fellside which is made up of a number of rounded summits with Cross Fell at 2930 feet (893 metres) being easily recognised as the highest. Because Cross Fell is not isolated as is Pendle or each of the Three Peaks above Ribblesdale it does not stand out in splendid isolation although it is still very impressive. Only the energetic walkers can easily reach the summit of Cross Fell from Alston and an even greater effort is required for the walk from the Upper Valley of the Tees. The rocks of the area consist of sandstones and shales although there are some areas of Carboniferous limestone. There are even older rocks hereabouts especially around Cronkley Scar. There are slates and ash which have been dated as over 400 million years old and some of these were exposed by geological upheavals and pencil slates were manufactured hereabouts in the 19th century. Teesdale, however, is dominated by the Great Whin Sill a hard quartz dolerite volcanic rock squeezed whilst still molten between layers of carboniferous rock around 250 million years ago. It is highly resistant to erosion, although there is plenty of evidence of the dramatic effect of the Teesdale glacier which flowed down the valley and as it melted left behind boulder clay, and glacial drift plus heaps of material known as drumlins.

Another village bounded by the River Eden is Dufton from which High Cup Nick can be visited. This natural amphitheatre is a good example of the effect of ice on rock and having a much more dramatic effect upon limestone but less effective on the harder volcanic rocks making up the great Whin Sill. The dominant high point in this area is Mickle Fell at 2591 feet (789 metres).

Beyond the true Pennines are three areas of interest for walkers of the long distance footpath, the Bewcastle Fells, Kielder Forest and finally the Cheviots (pronounced Cheeveots). The Bewcastle uplands are typical grouse moors dominated by areas of peat and heather and the highest point is Christianbury Crags at 1,598 feet (487 metres). Human interference has been much more obvious in and around what is now known as the Border Forest which covers 280 square miles and some 75,000 acres (30,000 hectares) of mainly conifers are organised by the Forestry Commission from their headquarters at Kielder Castle. Some remnants of the ancient deciduous woodland remains.

The Cheviots, situated to the north and feeding the pretty River Coquet, cover some 300 square miles which are dominated by the massive central dome of the Cheviot itself which reaches 2,676 feet (815 metres). Although not considered to be spectacular we find Cheviot to be a hauntingly attractive range made up of granite and other volcanic rocks worn smooth by the action of glaciers and with the flatter areas clothed with dark damp peat and drier areas of heather. The Cheviots are best explored from the market town of Wooler.

Obviously any upland area will be subject to extreme weather but on the other hand there are isolated areas protected from tramping feet. Birds and mammals will also find peace and quiet far from the madding crowds. Typical Pennine plants and found in few other areas, include the rare fern called moonwort, whilst other interesting plants include stemless thistle, cowberry, bilberry, bearberry and cloudberry. In limestone areas melancholy thistle, mountain pansy, lily of the valley, mezereon, bloody cranesbill and cowslip all thrive. Yew, small leaved lime and

The peregrine is a species found in the Pennines with its population showing a dramatic increase.

especially rowan are also typical. The rivers in these areas are also rich in aquatic life including mayfly and stonefly with many species of freshwater snail and mussel plus the increasingly rare crayfish which was once an important item of human food. Fish include the river lamprey, brown trout, miller's thumb also known as the bullhead, and in some Pennine rivers there are excellent runs of salmon and sea trout which is simply a migratory form of brown trout. Frogs and toads are both common with the slow worm the reptile most frequently seen. The bird life is rich in species but in some of the uplands they have to be searched for; merlins are rare and seem to be declining whilst the peregrine is also rare but their improvement has been spectacular throughout the 1980s and is continuing. Despite the unwelcome attentions of some gamekeepers whose opinions are out of date by more than a century the hen harrier has also shown a welcome increase since 1980. Breeding species include pied flycatcher, redstart which occur in the woodland areas whilst the moorland areas are the haunt of meadow pipit, skylark, wheatear, red grouse, lapwing, curlew and golden plover. Ravens are also a feature of the high fells. Dipper and grey wagtail are common residents along the Pennine rivers whilst they are joined in summer by sand martin and common sandpiper. Along some of the deeper reaches of the rivers kingfishers perch in the trees overhanging the water and dive in search of fish. The Pennines is the only area in England where the mountain hare occurs, having been introduced into Derbyshire and Saddleworth near Oldham during the late 19th century although a similar introduction around Pendle Hill proved unsuccessful. The species is also found in the Cheviots. Other mammals found in the Pennine area include the native otter and the North American mink which has escaped from fur farms and has devastated other forms of wildlife as it has no natural predator in Britain. Roe deer are common and native, red deer are uncommon and native whilst in the Bowland area on the outskirts of the Pennines sika deer occur which were introduced by Lord Ribblesdale in the mid 19th century and some of the escapees now live wild. Both the red fox and the brown hare are common in the Pennines and both are hunted, the badger is increasing rapidly following the protection given to this delightful animal. Red and grey squirrels both occur in the Pennines with the native red recovering after almost a century of worrying decline but the grey introduced from North America around 1870 has caused much damage to the other wildlife especially nesting birds. Foresters count the cost of damage to trees in terms of millions rather than thousands of pounds and grey squirrels have to be culled in some areas.

CHAPTER 2

The Derbyshire Peak

The Pennine Way begins around Edale and the once isolated village has thus gained fame. The Pennines themselves taper down towards central Derbyshire and thus southern peakland marks the end of the range. There is good walking around Eastmoor but there is no doubt that Edale is a perfect base from which to begin to discover the Pennines. It is usually the case that walkers prefer to follow the route from south to north rather than in the reverse direction. The accepted opinion is that both the sun and the prevailing bad weather is always at the back of the walker proceeding from south to north.

We arrived in Edale on a glorious morning in late May with the sun just beginning to evaporate the dew from the green grass and the sound of a cuckoo echoing from the natural amphitheatre in which the village is situated. Already the car park was filling and walkers of all shapes and sizes wearing apparel of every colour and style strode out purposefully in search of the high fells. Edale is sited in a remote valley tucked away between the two brooding hills of Mam Tor and Kinder Scout. It comes as rather a surprise to find a railway station here but Edale is situated between Sheffield and Manchester and thus kept firmly in touch with civilisation. Of all the Pennines the Derbyshire area is most under threat from the pressure of walkers as it is well within range of a day's visit by visitors from Manchester, Sheffield and the Midlands. Like the sound of the cuckoo the passage of trains reverberates through Edale and even human voices sound louder in this atmosphere. On the wall of the Old Nags Head Inn is a sign indicating the start of the Pennine Way and the hostelry's substantial bar snacks can provide energy for the beginning or sustenance at the end of a strenuous walk. Nearby is a National Park Information Centre featuring displays concerning the Pennine Way and other shorter footpaths and a regularly up-dated weather information board. A good selection of books, leaflets and postcards are on sale and it is possible to book here for space

The Old Nags Head at Edale at the southern end of the Pennine Way.

on the adjacent camp site. Here also is a mountain rescue post, which is vital during adverse weather conditions when far too many people take far too many risks. There are a couple of good cafes in the village including one next to the station and Coopers cafe which has a camp site behind it. The local church also organises residential accommodation. Edale is one of the few areas where tourists in muddy boots, carrying large packs and accompanied by dogs on leads are accepted as the norm — it is those wearing suits and dresses who look out of place. The food served hereabouts is both fresh and substantial.

For those interested in a day's walk there are two particularly good routes — up onto Kinder Scout and up to the summit of Mam Tor, the 'shivering mountain'. A walk along the winding paths to the summit of the latter is likely to result in contact with a number of hang gliders. Kinder Scout is a plateau some 15 square miles in area (39 sq. km) with steep sides and cloughs cut out by the clear cool water which has been working steadily away since the Ice Ages. Nearby rises the delightfully named River Dove which was made famous by Isaac Walton whose *Compleat Angler* is one of the finest books on fishing ever written, and although completed in the 1650s still has a modern ring to it. Once the summit is reached walkers must still keep their wits about them as the plateau consists of a great many muddy hollows called 'groughs' which are produced by the action of water on the soft peaty soil. These are not only interesting but also extremely dangerous and some 'groughs' can be more than 15 feet (4.5 metres) deep. The route follows the gritstone terraine over Kinder to Bleaklow an area which appears as white as snow when cotton grass reaches its flowering peak during July whilst later in the summer and early autumn the same area is purple with the heather and the air throbs with the buzzing of bees in search of the rich nectar. Eventually the Pennine Way descends towards the Snake Pass but this book, as already mentioned, is not about the footpath but the area. No one wanting to discover the Pennines can afford to miss Mam Tor or the attractive tourist village of Castleton which it overlooks, and which can be reached via Winnats Pass.

Winnats is a small yet startlingly dramatic pass between limestone hills and is thought to have been created by the collapse of the roof of a huge cave. This is an area of dramatic caves and the Speedwell Cavern to be described later stands at the entrance to the pass. The climb up Winnats is steep and it must have been an isolated spot until the development of powerful cars and these are now so numerous in the peak of the season that the National Trust, who administer the area, are sometimes obliged to restrict access. At the top of the pass the road to Buxton which is some ten miles away is signed. To the south west of the pass is Mam Tor which takes its name from the Celtic mam meaning a hill and there is an Iron Age hill fort on the summit and occupying an area of 16 acres (6.4 hectares). The National Trust own the site and during 1991 they carried out repair work to redress the damage done by thousands of interested feet. The first settlement on Mam Tor was probably around 1400 BC. From the summit which is composed of layers of shale and sandstone there are magnificent views down to the Hope Valley. The shale is so unstable that there are regular rock falls which accounts for the alternative name of Shivering mountain, at the foot of which is the Odin mine, one of the oldest lead mines in Britain.

Castleton itself caters well for visitors who flock to the area of castle and caves and although entry fees are required almost everywhere, there is no doubt that there is value for money. The secret here is not to rush — take your time and be sure

A delightful streamside path leads from Castleton to the Peak Cavern.

to visit Peveril Castle, each of the four caverns, the parish church of St Edmund, the Ollerenshaw museum of Blue John and outside the village St Peter's church at Hope and the Chestnut centre on the road to Chapel-en-le-Frith should not be missed.

Castleton is always busy but is bursting at the seams on Garland Day which probably originated as a pre-Christian fertility ceremony. After the restoration of Charles II following a period of Civil War and ten years of Cromwellian repression the date was changed from May 1 to May 29. This is 'Oak apple day' which commemorates Charles II hiding in an oak tree in 1651 to escape from Cromwell's forces, this being followed by his escape to France and subsequent restoration. The Garland itself is made from wild flowers and is said to weigh more than 50 pounds — it certainly swamps the 'king' who wears it over his head as he is paraded, along with his consort, through the village. At the end of the ceremony the garland is hoisted by rope to the top of the church tower.

The ruins of Peveril Castle dominate Castleton and indeed accounts for its name and it was founded as early as 1086. Some, but not all, historians have suggested that William Peveril was the illegitimate son of William the Conqueror and he was given several other large manors in addition to Castleton. Sir Walter Scott, who travelled widely in the Pennines, found the mystery of William Peveril irresistible and used a great deal of poetic licence plus a few facts to write *Peverel of the Peak*, perhaps mis-spelling the name to ensure that his work, which was published in 1823, was regarded as fiction. It is likely that Scott changed the spelling of the name to ensure his readers were aware that the plot was fictional, although for centuries the pile was known as the Peak Castle, and the village grew up under and was protected by it. The Peverils did not hold on to their property for very long because in 1155 they were involved in the poisoning of a favourite of the King and their lands were forfeited to the Crown. Thus most of the present buildings still standing within the complex were not actually built by the Peverils, but the masons were all good at their job. Now under the care of English Heritage we have one of the few substantial Norman buildings to be found in Derbyshire. After passing through the paybox which also sells guides and

The church of St. Edmund, Castleton.

postcards, a spiralling path leads to the castle and there are splendid views to the town below both from the castle walls and from the path itself. Behind the castle and reached via a footpath from the market square is Cave Dale, a very attractive walk with many an ideal spot for a quiet picnic. For those who need more help to discover the delights of the area then a residential visit to Losehill Hall outside Castleton is a good idea. It was opened by the Peak National Park's Planning Board and the Countryside Commission in 1972. Beautifully sited in the Hope valley the centre organises courses throughout the year, many with an environmental bias.

Like all limestone regions the area around Castleton is honeycombed with caverns produced by the effect of rain water on the rocks. The first chemistry lesson given to children is to drop acid onto chips of limestone which fizzes as it dissolves and gives off carbon dioxide gas. Rain water is a dilute solution of carbonic acid and over many thousands of years huge caverns have been produced, richer seams of valuable and more resistant rocks and minerals exposed, and phenomenal shapes and colours created. The caves, like those in Derbyshire and also in Ribblesdale and the Craven Dales, were once used as shelter by long extinct animals such as the woolly rhinocerous, mammoth, bear, sabre toothed tiger and reindeer. All these species were ideally suited to the cold conditions present as the ice retreated and the climate altered. The limestone, as we have already seen, is an indication that prior to this time this area of Derbyshire lay beneath a warm shallow sea, rich in invertebrate life.

The advantage of the Castleton Caves over those in some other areas is that they are close together, and although all four major systems have their own car parks they can be reached by walking from the village itself. The closest is the Peak Cavern reached by following a delightful riverside path bordered by colourful cottages and gardens beneath the towering cliff on top of which stands Peveril Castle. In spring and summer the approach to the cave entrance is a botanical treat with dog's mercury, wood sorrel, celandine and bluebell among the many common species whilst throughout the year are found several species of fern including the attractive hart's tongue. Above on the ledges of the cliff are resident jackdaws whose echoing calls of 'Jack-Daw Jack-Daw' are just as easily onamatopaeic as that of the cuckoo.

At the entrance to the Peak Cavern, which was once rudely called 'The Devil's Arse' and said to be the second largest cave opening in the world, is guarded by a cafe, shop and pay-box with the overhangs and colourful umbrellas producing an alpine effect as well as much needed protection from the often unreliable weather. The interior is well lit and once contained a small working village; there is still ample evidence of the houses and also a pub with the blackened roof of the cave a reminder of the fires which once crackled in the hearths. The inhabitants made their living from making rope and some of their equipment has been preserved. When Moritz was travelling through the Pennines in 1782 he noted 'to the right in the hollow of the cavern, a whole subterranean village where the inhabitants, on account of it being Sunday, were resting from their work and with happy and cheerful looks were sitting at the doors of their huts.'

Guided tours are provided every 15 minutes or so, as is the case with the Speedwell Cavern although the contrast between the two could hardly be greater and it is certainly not possible

The Speedwell Cavern is sited at the entrance to the narrow Winnats Pass.

to say of these caves that once you have seen one you have seen them all. Speedwell is explored by boat which conveys passengers along half a mile of illuminated chambers, with an embarcation at the furthest point at Bottomless Pit Cavern. There must certainly be a bottom to it but none have yet plumbed it and the views above of the shiny damp rocks are equally awe inspiring. For once in the bowels of the Speedwell we were sorry that it was impossible to proceed further and at last understood what it is that spurs on cavers to make one more effort to push into the unknown.

The Treak Caverns are about half a mile west of the village and here is the only workable vein of Blue John one of the rarest minerals of its type and which local craftsmen fashion into attractive jewelry and ornaments which are sold in almost all the village shops. There is a fine display of Blue John at the Ollerenshaw Museum on Castleton's main street and for which there is a small entry fee. Treak Cavern is entered through the same tunnel used by the old miners, the first excavations to be seen being the Old Series followed by other caverns only discovered in 1926 and called the New Series. Discoveries in the Treak in 1923 have proved that the mines may well have been occupied during the Bronze Age because skeletons were discovered along with flint artefacts. The urgent demand for flourspar, used to make a flux required in steel making during the First World War destroyed much of the Blue John and the cave only opened to the public in 1935. Expertly illuminated it offers some of the most spectacular cave scenery to be found anywhere in the world and the series well earn such names as Dream Cave, Aladdin's Cave and our favourite the Witch's Cave so named because the lighting throws a shadow resembling an old crone on her broomstick.

The fourth cavern open to the public is the Blue John Cave, equally as impressive as the others and made famous by Sir Arthur Conan Doyle in his tale of *'The Terror of the Blue John Gap'*. Blue John itself is an ore of zinc, but there is some difference of opinion regarding the origin of the name. The miners certainly called a darker form of zinc ore 'Black Jack' and it is logical to suppose that the prettier form would be referred to as 'Blue John'. Another possibility is that the ore was once in demand in France and its blue and yellow consistency was called 'bleu jaune' which the English workers tried to pronounce properly but only managed 'Blue John'. Whatever the origin of the name there is no disputing that the mineral has been in demand for centuries and vases made from Blue John have been found among the ashes of Pompeii near Naples which was wiped out when Mount Etna erupted in AD 79. Only small ornaments can now be made from the remaining deposits and it is no longer possible to fashion the delightful vases such as the example to be seen at Chatsworth House. The Blue John Cave itself has a less imposing entrance than the others but once the steep steps have been negotiated what glories are to be found and once again they have been illuminated to bring out the best features. The Waterfall Cavern has an effect created by hundreds of stalactites fused together to produce a wave effect. Stalactite has a c in it and so does a ceiling from which they hang; in contrast stalagmite has a g in it and so does the ground from which they grow. There is also the so-called Lord Mulgrave's dining room where the said gentleman who loved the caves used to provide a banquet for the 19th-century miners who allowed him to explore the area without hinderance. Anyone planning a trip around Castleton should visit the Castleton Village Museum which is situated opposite a garage on Buxton Road. It opens on most days throughout the summer and is well worth the small entry fee.

Hope church is dedicated to St. Peter.

There are exhibits on lead mining, rope making, geology and especially the history of the Garland Day Ceremony.

The Church of St. Edmund, although not mentioned in Domesday, was almost certainly founded by the Peverils, although its dedication does hint at an even earlier origin. Edmund was an East Anglian King who died in a deluge of Danish arrows as he sought to defend his Christian faith against the heathen. Only bits of the Norman stonework now remains following an almost complete restoration in 1837 although a fine set of personally inscribed box pews were retained as was a piscina in which the vessels used in the pre-Reformation Catholic mass were washed. Another interesting feature of the church is its library, a feature more typical of large city cathedrals rather than small village parish churches. Castleton's library was established by the Rev Frederick Farran who was vicar here for 37 years and on his death left around 600 volumes which could be loaned by parishioners 'at the discretion of the minister'. Not all the texts were religious and included are the works of Samuel Johnson, Clarendon's Rebellion; religious tomes were, however, obviously an important part of the vicar's library and there is a 1539 copy of Cranmer's Great Bible and also a so called Breeches Bible of 1611 in which the aprons produced to hide Adam and Eve's modesty were referred to as 'breeches'.

At nearby Hope church dedicated to St Peter there is also a Breeches Bible on display, but also a Vinegar Bible, another 17th-century misprint which records the parable of the vineyard as the parable of the vinegar. The Breeches Bible once belonged to the Rev Thomas Bocking who also taught school and his schoolmaster's chair is dated 1664 and bears a Latin inscription which when translated reads 'You cannot make a scholar out of twisted wood.' Hope means a valley and there was a church here in Saxon times; nothing remains of the original church but there is part of a Saxon cross in the church. There was a Roman fort at Hope and a road ran to Glossop where there was also a fort and it passed close to the modern A57 road over Snake Pass and the Pennine Way itself. This ancient stretch of road is now called Doctors Gate. The Snake Pass climbs up from the Derwent valley, skirts Kinder Scout and is said to take its name not because it twists and turns up and down the hill

A fine example of a 9th century Anglo-Saxon Cross in Hope churchyard.

but from the Snake Inn. The Dukes of Devonshire owned the area and the snake is part of their coat of arms.

From the Snake Pass the route down into Glossop is pleasant in summer but can be terrifying after winter snow. It is an ideal place from which to explore the river valleys of the Etherow, Derwent and Goyt. It would be so easy to drive straight through

The complex of Woodhead tunnels which are now, alas closed, and a chapter in Pennine transport history is over.

Glossop and write it off as yet another town with its origins firmly set in the Industrial Revolution. By following the signs to Old Glossop and also visiting the Visitors' Centre on the forecourt of the railway station the town changes character and looks what it once was — an important market centre on the site of a Roman fort. This was known either as Melandra which was the local name, although Scholars prefer the original name of Ardotolia. The few remains of the buildings are set on a hill overlooking the junction of the little Glossop Brook with the more substantial River Etherow. There is a picnic area based on the site. Lying under the protection of the

Norman parish church is Old Glossop which has some fine 17th and 18th-century cottages dominated by a market cross. Initially modern Glossop was called Howard Town. Many towns describe themselves as the entrance to somewhere but Glossop's claim to be the Gateway to the Peak would seem to be more deserved than some. It is certainly the key to the discovery of rivers which rise on the Peak.

The Etherow flows through Longdendale and has played a major rôle in the development of the region ever since the time of the Romans and probably well before this. The area has a strange geography since a finger of Cheshire pushes into Longendale but being artificially created by the powerful Earls of Chester who wished to have the valuable salt road under their control. The old route into Yorkshire crossed Salter's Brook. In 1838 work began on the first Woodhead Tunnel financed by the Sheffield, Ashton-under-Lyne and Manchester Railway Company. It was 3 miles 13 yards long and at that time twice the length of any previous tunnel in the world. It was the 19th-century equivalent of the Channel Tunnel. The first tunnel was replaced by a second in 1852 and public access is not allowed to either. A third rail tunnel was constructed in 1954 and the second remained idle until 1963 when the Peak District National Park prevented the crest of the Pennines from having to carry electric pylons and destroying the views. The cables are carried through the tunnel which has a maintenance line running through it. In the late 1980s the rail link was closed and the Etherow valley no longer echoes to the sound of engines. This is a shame, for what a boon it would have been for the tourists, especially if steam locomotives were used.

The 'long-dale' is a V-shaped valley receiving water from the slopes of Bleaklow which just tops 2000 feet (609 metres) and Black Hill which almost reaches the same height. The annual rainfall exceeds 50 inches (125 cms) and thus the area was an ideal choice for the siting of reservoirs and in 1877 the Etherow was impounded into five reservoirs at Bottoms, Valehouse, Rhodeswood, Torside and Woodhead. These provided essential water for the textile towns of Cheshire as the Industrial Revolution gathered pace and developed an insatiable thirst. Wildlife has adapted surprisingly well to these reservoirs and in winter birdwatchers enjoy many an exciting day with species

Ladybower reservoir used for angling, boating, birdwatching and water sports as well as to provide water for domestic and industrial use.

such as mallard, tufted duck, pochard, goosander and teal plus both Bewick and whooper swans. Coot, grey heron, great crested grebe and dabchick are also found on all the reservoirs. At the time of their construction the reservoirs were the largest and most dangerous civil engineering project the world had ever seen. In descriptions of the Pennines their brief flirtation with Cheshire is often not mentioned but the prosperity of the county was built on the supply of water from the uplands. Despite these extractions the vegetation of Upper Longdendale has remained of interest. The uplands are composed mainly of gritstone with areas of mudstone and soft shale. Initially the area was dominated by woodland with oak, elm, rowan and birch all present; the odd remnant of this ancient forest remains but has been diluted by planting of alien conifers including spruce and larch. A period of harsh climate, however, produced moorlands dominated by rough grass, heather and mosses growing on a blanket of peat. This is suitable habitat for short tailed field vole, fox, rabbit and both the brown and mountain hare. Birds include curlew, golden plover, ring ouzel and here is one of the best areas for studying the twite which is often referred to as the mountain linnet. There are records in most years of osprey passing through usually in May and another very unusual visitor was a Manx shearwater blown this far inland by high winds. All five species of British owl occur in Longdendale namely the barn, long-eared, short eared, little and tawny. Merlins breed on the highlands, part of which are still managed for red grouse.

The Upper Derwent Valley has been subjected to the same method of development this time to provide Derby, Nottingham, Leicester and Sheffield on the opposite side of the Pennine chain. Three reservoirs, the Howden, Derwent and Ladybower together make up a six mile chain of water which are used to provide a variety of recreational activities as well as their main function of providing essential water. The Howden and Derwent reservoirs, together occupying 336 acres (134·4 hectares) were built between 1901 and 1906, with Ladybower itself having an area of 502 acres (250 hectares), being built between 1935 and 1945. Its shores are thickly wooded and have picnic areas and there are plenty of well marked footpaths around all three reservoirs. The drive beyond the

A typical Pennine scene — Goyt Bridge is a popular tourist spot.

huge Ladybower Dam across open moorland has often proved too popular and access is restricted during the summer and at weekends. Beyond Howden reservoir towards Slipperden is a 17th-century packhorse bridge which was moved and rebuilt as the Ladybower reservoir was being constructed. It is dedicated to John Derry who was a Sheffield-based journalist who wrote a number of informative guide books to the area.

The third of the river valleys is the Goyt and this has also been subjected to reservoir mania; together with the other Pennine rivers of Etherow and Tame the Goyt is a major tributary to the Mersey which they form at Stockport. In June 1989 we spent a week in the area making a film for Channel IV television about pollution of northern rivers.

The Goyt begins life in the soft boggy uplands just beyond the Cat and Fiddle Inn which is at 1,689 feet (515 metres) above sea level and the second highest pub in England. In summer the beautiful Goyt bridge, once part of a cross-Pennine packhorse route, is such a popular spot that a one way system has had to be devised to keep the traffic moving. Apart from walkers this is curlew and sheep country with the stream being clean and fast running. Biologically it is classified as Grade 1A which means that it is perfectly clean. Insect larvae of both stoneflies and mayflies are typical of such regions. From this point well above Buxton and Macclesfield the Goyt feeds down first into the Errwood and then the Fernilee reservoir which was constructed later. Before these were constructed to slake the thirst of Stockport in the last century, the Goyt would have tumbled down towards Whaley Bridge. Even before the reservoirs came there was plenty of industrial activity in the area, and below the waters of Fernilee lie the remains of a gunpowder works which was closed in the 1920s. From the dam, water is sluiced down to the treatment works, where the drinking water is tested and if necessary treated with chlorine to destroy bacteria or caustic soda to neutralise the naturally acidic water. North West Water is also obliged to provide compensation water to ensure the flow of the Goyt which it does to the extent of 13.6 megalitres (3 million gallons) per day. At this point we still have a class 1A river but what happens between Taxal Bridge and Whaley Bridge is a source of great controversy. Any river can be classified according to the number of species of aquatic organisms found in it and of course their respective populations. Insect larvae, which are easily and quickly identified form the major part of the diet of fish particularly trout and also of some birds particularly the dipper. The presence of these insects is affected by the

A typical Pennine reservoir at Foulridge near Colne used as a roost by wildfowl including Canada Geese.

amount of dissolved oxygen in the water and also by poisonous effluents. When these disappear the fish which depend upon them are also unable to survive. When a river changes from grade 1 to grade 2 the amenity value of the river is not badly affected. Typical of Grade 2 rivers is Asellus a crustacean also known as the water louse. But the Goyt suddenly drops to a grade 4 when few if any organisms can survive and this decline is due to one thing — industry! This happens around the little town of Whaley Bridge which finds itself in something of a dilemma. Local bleachworks employ more than 400 people and whilst the owners try to control their effluent it does make parts of the Goyt unfit to play any part in the tourist development of the area. Things are improving and another bit of goods news for Pennine discoverers is the Peak Forest Canal where there is a well used footpath called 'A walk between the Two Navvies!'. This involves following the canal tow path from the Navigation Arms situated just above the canal at Whaley Bridge to an inn of the same name at Bugsworth. From Whaley Bridge the towpath leads beneath the new A6 bypass, passing a footpath down to the confluence of Black Brook and the River Goyt. During the 1970s the Bugsworth Navigation Inn was owned by the actress

Pat Phoenix, famous for her rôle as Elsie Tanner in Coronation Street. The canal basin is being restored as nearly as possible to its 1920 condition and has been sensibly designated as an ancient monument. This is the attitude prevailing in almost every section of the Pennines at the present time and where there is a sensible tendency to balance the needs of industry and the employment it provides with an appreciation for the conservation of both history and wildlife. This has certainly been the case in the South Pennines which divide the cotton towns of Lancashire from the woollen centres of Yorkshire.

CHAPTER 3

The South and West Pennines

The Derbyshire Peak District and the Yorkshire Dales have been part of our tourist landscape for many years. Both have been given National Park status and who knows if the South Pennines which is sandwiched between them may sometime in the future be granted a similar status.

We have lived in and around the South Pennines for many years but the new name took us by surprise as indeed did the West Pennine Moors which branches out from it, including Rossendale and Pendle.

In 1967 the Calder Civic Trust put forward the idea of a Park and by 1974 the name South Pennine Park was being applied to the area from Standedge bordering the Peak National Park and running to the area around Skipton often referred to as the Gateway to the Yorkshire Dales.

We regard Holmfirth as the key to this area of the Pennines, having its origins as a village based upon the production of wool, which took the Industrial Revolution in its stride and has recently made more than a good living from the tourist industry. Now at the heart of Kirklees, West Yorkshire, Holmfirth has tea rooms, craft shops and a market with Sunday being one of its busiest days. Initial prosperity was based upon the excellence of its woollen yarns and cloth first produced in the three storeyed cottages is still very much a part of the village. Later the mills were powered by the River Holme which was, however, subject to flooding especially in the years 1977, 1852 and 1944; the 1852 deluge was by far the worst due to the bursting of the dam of Bilberry Reservoir when more than 80 people were drowned plus large numbers of farm animals, whilst the damage to property was almost total in some areas. Tourists now flood into the village its fame being well known as the set for the classic television comedy *The Last of the Summer Wine*. Actually Holmfirth almost became Britain's equivalent to Hollywood in the days of the silent movies. This is faithfully recorded in the Holmfirth Postcard Museum which is open

Pennine winters can be harsh as this view in the Pendleside village of Roughlee in the middle of Witch country well shows.

Monday to Saturday 10 am to 5 pm and on Sundays from 1pm to 5 pm. Bamfords of Holmfirth made their reputation with the production of saucy seaside postcards but were also involved in the production of lantern slides, song and hymn sheets and silent movies.

There always seems to be something going on at Holmfirth which is only a couple of miles from the Peak District and therefore the ideal bridge into the South Pennines; craft market and shops abound, there is a folk festival in the second week of May, sheepdog trials in early July and a candlelight procession early in September. For those without cars there are regular bus services from Glossop, Huddersfield and to a gaggle of delightful little Pennine villages including Netherthong, Upperthong, Wooldale, Holme and Honley the latter having its village centre designated as a site of historic interest.

Geologically the South Pennines were formed around 350 million years ago when the climate was much warmer and wetter with the natural rocks covered by a shallow sea which were described in chapter one.

The human lifespan is very short and it is hard for us to imagine the vast scale of geological time, but if we could speed

The authors with their labrador Bono close to their home beneath Pendle Hill.

this process up it would be possible to see the area now occupied by the South Pennines as a shallow basin of sea into which poured fast moving rivers carrying large volumes of grit and sand. These too were deposited and formed the stone so typical of this area and which is known as sandstone and gritstone. These coarse stones were much later found to be ideal for grinding corn and became known as millstone grit or just plain gritstone, an ideal building material so well known to those interested in the vernacular architecture of the textile towns of Yorkshire and Lancashire.

Eventually some life forms left the sea and vegetation covered the land and imposed its impact on the landscape of the area. In the estuarine area a forest of huge ferns some as large as the trees of the modern tropical rain forests became dominant. As these huge swathes of vegetation died they fell into the swampy land and became compressed into coal seams between areas of gritstone. This accounts for the coal industry which until very recently was an important part of the economy of the South Pennines. Most of the mines have now been worked out, but in 1989 we made a television film about a privately owned pit near Cliviger and one of us descended on a tiny bogie into the depths of a drift mine. Here the tough colliers, who are paid according to the volume of coal they produce, told us that they often found fossils and during the time we were with them they produced several fine examples. Some fossil plants became embedded in the sandstone and shales and these often come to light when rock is quarried. Huge tree ferns including Calamites and Lepidodendron have been found in such places, especially at Foster Clough near Mytholmroyd.

Initially this complex geological formation was part of a massive continent covering the bulk of the northern hemisphere, but deep seated movements of the earth split the land and the part which is now the Pennines were pushed up and became folded. The axis, as any Pennine walker knows was roughly in a north-south direction descending quite steeply on the western side, but sloping much more gently towards the east. But there was also a second fold which resulted in the formation of the Rossendale Hills and Pendle with the Burnley to Colne basin sandwiched between them. From Pendle there is a second basin now occupied by Clitheroe and beyond this rises yet another upland area of the Bowland Fells. Once more this region was ideal for the construction of reservoirs to provide domestic, industrial and canal compensation water.

There has always been rivalry between Lancashire and Yorkshire and the only time the two unite is when either is threatened by anyone from another county. South Pennine Park should also do much to unite the two as the area is reached from the mill towns straddling the borders between the two counties.

Standedge is a moorland ridge straddling the boundary between the Peak National Park and the South Pennine Park and here the Pennine Way crosses both areas. This area of dark peaty moor had an even more ancient trackway and at Castleshaw on a slight rise are the outlines of a Roman fort —

The art of hedging lives on, in the area around the West Pennine Moors and the Trough of Bowland.

Dunsop Bridge village is the perfect base from which to explore the Bowland Fells.

or to be strictly accurate two forts one inside the other. At the low lying area below the old fort there are now two little reservoirs. The inner fort originally occupied just over half an acre, the larger being about three acres. Archaeologists have discovered roads leading into the fort complex and ramparts made of sods of grass towering over a ditch. Pottery and coins dated to the first century AD and so has a tile lettered COH 111 BRE. The remains of a hypercaust has also been excavated and because similar things have been found at Manchester, Slack, and Richmond it is suggested that Castleshaw was built on the orders of Agricola between AD 79 and 80.

From Standedge the Pennine Way leads to the Readycon Gap where there is yet another small reservoir which many writers have described as rather like a lakeland tarn and as Cumbrians we can clearly see their reasoning. Nearby is Rapes Highway which is an easily recognisable section of the old packhorse route which ran from Rochdale to Marsden. A battle royal was fought in 1908 when new roads were being planned and rights of way were threatened. The developers were of the opinion that the packhorse routes as described in chapter four were no longer needed. Walkers and conservationists were looked upon as cranks — fortunately the cranks won. A lasting memorial to their efforts is the packhorse bridge at Marsden which is known as Eastergate Bridge.

Not too long ago the Pennine walker in these parts would have felt to have been on the edge of the civilised world but in the 1970s there came a rude awakening in the form of the M62 motorway. Those of us who enjoy discovering Britain should never complain about developments which keep the tourist routes quiet enough to explore. There are several points on the Pennine trail which must be visited and Blackstone Edge is one such point. It is one of the highest points in the southern pennines and at 1550 feet (472 metres) and from it the views are magnificent. Some 300 feet (91.4 metres) below lie a tangle of rocks left behind as the glaciers retreated and melted at the conclusion of the last Ice Age and these upland areas were home to Neolithic settlers and their flint artefacts have frequently been discovered and are now on display in the museums of Rochdale, Oldham, Halifax and Huddersfield. Crossing the Edge is the so called Roman road. Whether this is the case or whether it is a packhorse track has caused academic argument but Castleshaw camp is close by and the actual construction of the route could well be Roman. Whatever the truth of the matter the trackway is ancient and interesting as are all the trans-Pennine communications which are the subject of the next chapter.

Some mention must first be made here, however, of an even older trackway which links Hebden Bridge and Heptonstall with Burnley and is known as the Long Causeway. The route was almost certainly Neolithic in origin although it was 'improved' as the packhorse trade evolved. Erosion was a problem and the horses hooves gouged out what was literally 'a hollow way' which is obviously the origin of the Holloway road in London. To preserve these routes large stones called causeys were laid to produce a causeway. As with the Blackstone Edge area there have been numerous neolithic tools and artefacts found along the Long Causeway, usually above the 1300 feet (396 metres) contour, above the wet boggy valley bottoms.

Travellers from Burnley into Calderdale know the winding sweep of the Long Causeway well although first time visitors

Countryside Wardens are now a welcome sight to Pennine walkers.

are often confused because there are two River Calders. The Lancashire Calder rises above Todmorden and flows through Burnley to meet the Ribble at Whalley and thence to the west coast beyond Preston. The Yorkshire Calder rises close by and runs through Hebden Bridge, Sowerby Bridge, Wakefield and then on to the Humber estuary and the east coast. For some of its journey the Lancashire Calder follows the line of the Leeds to Liverpool canal, whilst the Yorkshire Calder meanders around the Rochdale Canal. These canals are described in the next chapter.

Within the context of the South Pennines there are some outlying areas which should be considered including the Rossendale moors, Pendleside and Bowland which together form a western arm to the range and there is an increasing tendency to refer to these simply as the West Pennines.

The West Pennine Moors were opened up during the 1980s with the establishment of a number of Information Centres particularly at the Great House Barn at Rivington near Horwich close to Bolton, Jumbles Country Park at Bradshaw also near Bolton, Clough Head at Haslingden in Rossendale, and Roddlesworth at Tockholes between Darwen and Blackburn. No wonder local naturalists were up in arms when a government backed scheme proposed to plant huge areas of moorland with alien conifers. Thankfully the scheme was rejected and these areas are now quite safe from future exploitation. A perfect way to see these hills without getting too tired is to travel by the East Lancashire Steam Railway which since 1991 has run between Bury and Rawtenstall. In the summer of 1991 one of Rossendale's famous industries — shoemaking — which still survives, celebrated its heritage by the opening of a museum at Gaghills Mill in Waterfoot. It reflects the history of slipper and shoe manufacture from the 1870s to the present day. The firm started by Sir Henry Trickett still produces five million pairs of shoes and slippers and employs more than 1,300 people in Waterfoot, Burnley and also on the Isle of Man. There are an increasing number of museums hereabouts including a textile exhibition at Helmshore and a private museum in Bacup run by the local Natural History and Photographic Society and known affectionately as 'The Nats!' At Whittaker Park in Rossendale the museum specialises in Pennine history and natural history, whilst there is one of the best collections of Tariff Boards from the many toll houses along the Pennine foothills. A number of these toll houses still stand, including one at Barrowford which forms part of the Pendle Heritage Centre which is also close to the Leeds to Liverpool canal. It sells leaflets including a long distance footpath based around Pendle Hill whose 1831 feet (558 metres) summit dominates this outlying arm of the Pennines. Pendle is often described as

Despite other industries sheep farming remains vital to the Pennine economy.

gaunt, brooding unfriendly and full of witches. True enough the Pendle Witch trials of 1612 still pursuade tourists to see strange shapes and imagine that Old Demdike and Mother Chattox can cause things to go bump in the night. We have lived between Roughlee and Newchurch for many years and outside our front door is a witches stone which the previous occupant told us must not be removed. We do not believe in witches but prefer to leave our stone unturned. Pendle, however, with its string of delightful villages including Barley where there is a Country Park, Downham, Pendleton, Wiswell and Sabden, is a delight and the rhyme chanted by the local children is more a picture of the hill than the witch stones.

Oh Pendle, oh Pendle, majestic, sublime,
Thy praises shall ring till the end of all time.

Towneley Park museum in Burnley, which is freely open to the public although closed on Saturdays, displayed a photograph during the summer of 1991 which set the literary world alight with surprise and enthusiasm. Mrs Audrey Hall discovered a photograph of Charlotte Brontë prior to which only one other was known and this is in the National Portrait gallery in London. This one should stay in the Pennines to celebrate the life of the area's greatest writer. Beyond Pendle, snuggled between it and the Trough of Bowland, is the market town of Clitheroe with its Norman keep standing proudly on top of a knoll of limestone. All these areas are fully described in our companion volume in this series *Inland Lancashire*. The paths and the countryside are looked after by a well organised Ranger Service. In contrast to many Pennine areas Bowland has more ancient hedgerows although it does have its share of stone walls. It is not uncommon to find hedgers at work; there is nothing to compare with the sound and sight of a hedger's fire unless it is the smell of bacon sizzling in a pan over the hot ashes.

The whole of the Southern Pennines is wonderful walking country with many paths following ancient green paths, Roman roads, packhorse routes or early turnpikes some of which are still used whilst others, long deserted, are already grassed over. These and other routes through the Pennines are the subject of the next chapter.

CHAPTER 4

Trans-Pennine Transport

As with any mountain range, crossing the Pennines has always been a problem and this was brought into sharp focus in the area separating Lancashire and Yorkshire as the Industrial Revolution developed. Large trading centres demanded good communications and a good way to explore this area of the Pennines is by following the old road, canal and railway routes.

Before the Turnpikes developed roads were a nightmare, especially after heavy rain which is so much a feature of the Pennines. Initially the tracks simply followed the line of the drove roads linking grazing areas, which were often in Scotland, to the important market centres in the south of England. The most influential of these is the South Pennine Packhorse Tracks Trust whose aim is to restore to use as public rights of way these ancient highways and offer opportunities for those who wish to explore them on horseback, mountain bike or on foot. Hereabouts the first stone causeways were built in the Middle Ages and strengthened the old Saxon tracks linking Whalley, Clitheroe, Kirkstall, Wakefield, Pontefract and Rochdale. Sadly many have already been destroyed during quarrying and mining activities and reservoir construction. The sections still remaining should be preserved with the same energy as would be devoted to a church or an old abbey. The Packhorse Inn on Widdop Moor between Burnley and Hebden Bridge is sited almost on the Pennine Way. It was built in 1610 at 970 feet (290 metres) and should be preserved as a monument of a bygone age. As other trades developed goods were transported by teams of packhorses and their tracks were eventually replaced by more modern roads; in the Southern Pennines new roads were more difficult to build than in lowland areas and the packhorse routes therefore survived longer. Recently societies have been established to preserve these old tracks and the lovely hump-backed bridges which crossed the little streams so typical of upland places. Many of the packhorses were bred

The packhorse bridge at Wycoller with the hall known to the Brontes in the background. The trail led via Haworth to the Piece Hall at Halifax.

in Galloway, and many of the driven cattle also came from the rich fields of south west Scotland.

What repairs were done in the old days had to be paid for by the parish through which they passed. During the monastic period it was in the interest of the monks to keep their trade routes open, but after the abbeys had been dissolved by Henry VIII their roads fell into an irreversible decline. The Highway Act of 1555 stipulated that all male parishoners had to work for six days each year without pay to repair the roads. Naturally many objected to this on the grounds that those who travelled the roads ought to pay for their upkeep. This was the philosophy behind the development of turnpike roads. When the concept of guarding the new roads with a toll gate developed is not known for certain, but there is a document which refers to tolls being levied in London to repair the road between Temple Bar and St Giles. During the Middle Ages many towns charged visitors crossing their bridge and used the revenue to cover the repairs to their span. This was certainly the case in Monmouth as long ago as 1296 but the idea of placing tolls on roads did not gather momentum until the late 18th century but the Pennines were slow to develop such roads. Early road builders included John Gott and Abraham Rhodes but there were three men with special skills. These were Thomas Telford (1757–1837) John Metcalfe (1717–1810) otherwise known as 'Blind Jack of Knaresborough' and John Loudon Macadam (1756–1836). The last two engineers were responsible for the construction of many of the south Pennine turnpikes, and although Telford is best known as a bridge builder it was he who masterminded the route from London to Holyhead which did so much to speed up communications with Ireland. John Metcalfe was in many ways the most remarkable of all road engineers as he was left blind following an attack of smallpox when he was only six. He was among the first to realise that only roads made of smooth stone could survive wheeled traffic. Before his fame as a road builder Metcalfe had earned a living as a fish dealer, pedlar, horse seller and also as a packhorse trader and waggoner. He thus realised that the roads were always difficult and sometimes impossible and he decided to do something about it. His method involved beating the earth flat and then laying flat blocks of stone on top. He filled in the cracks between the blocks with stone chippings, and he also cambered his roads to allow water to drain off into ditches. Macadam also used a cambered surface but his method was cheaper because he used only local stone the size of which diminished gradually from foundations to surface. The use of molten tar came much later. Macadam thus pleased the shareholders and the revenue collected from the toll houses was more likely to find its way into the coffers of the speculators. Many of these toll houses still stand throughout the Pennines as do the milestones which had to be placed to ensure that travellers were allowed to travel a fair distance for their toll. Finding these mile markers proves that the road was once a turnpike and adds fun to any journey. We can vouch for the fact that it keeps children quiet, indeed engrossed, during a Pennine journey.

Even when roads improved they were still far too bumpy to allow the reliable transportation of some goods especially delicate china and very heavy ore and coal. Far better to send these by inland waterways and it was even thought worth the effort to punch canals through the Southern Pennines

Tracks like this near Pils Mill at Bacup have long gone, but steps are now being taken to preserve the old Pennine routes.

or physically lift them over the hills. Three trans-Pennine waterways were built during the late 18th and early 19th centuries — the Leeds to Liverpool, the Huddersfield Narrow and the Rochdale canals.

At 127¼ miles the Leeds to Liverpool is the longest trans-Pennine canal and is still open throughout the whole of its length. It links Liverpool and the River Mersey with Leeds and the Yorkshire Calder and thence via the Humber to the North Sea. The original plan was to link with the Ribble around Clitheroe, but in the late 1760s the cotton towns on the Lancashire side of the Pennines and the Liverpool merchants insisted on a change of route to take in Burnley, Accrington, Blackburn, Chorley and Wigan. These towns were described in our companion volume *Discovering Inland Lancashire*. This present book describes the journey from Leeds to Skipton, the birthplace of Lady Anne Clifford, whose life was so integrated with Pennine history and who is described in Chapter 8.

Opened on 4 July 1777 a canal wharf was opened in the centre of Leeds and from here there is still a working link into the Aire-Calder navigation which has been open since the early 18th century. A substantial part of Pennine history can be studied by following the canal route to Skipton via Armley Mills, Kirkstall Abbey, Saltaire and Bingley and Keighley.

Armley Mills is one of the finest museums and is an informative day out for the whole family and well worth the entry fee. It is situated on an artificial triangle of land between the River Aire and the canal. A mill has been present here since 1559 when a corn mill was constructed and this was later adapted as a fulling mill which in 1788 became the largest such complex in the world and owned by William Gott. In 1804 the mill burned down but Gott could not afford it to be idle and it was soon replaced using the power of the Aire which had a weir constructed for the purpose. The most modern techniques of the age were developed at Armley and it is fitting that this mill has been chosen to house the City of Leeds' industrial museum. Here is an excellent exhibition of life on the canal, the history of cloth making and also aspects of the social life of the area. There is a fully operational cinema typical of the 1930s and outside there are a number of steam locomotives and machinery plus a surprisingly secluded picnic site. The museum is seen at its best on days when children dress in Victorian costume and play the rôle of textile operatives.

Another museum also situated close to both the canal and the River Aire is at Kirkstall Abbey. Kirkstall has been described as 'the finest early Cistercian abbey in this country' and although we would prefer to use the word 'was' rather than 'is', there is no doubt that it takes the prize for survival. The grounds were sliced in two by an early turnpike which is now the A65 road and has recently been cleaned of centuries of industrial grime. Kirkstall was founded as a daughter house of Fountains Abbey and its brethren had first tried to establish themselves at Barnoldswick before finding success at Kirkstall. Because there was plenty of good stone available locally the abbey was built very quickly and many of the structures dating to 1182 still stand. When Henry VIII began to dissolve the monasteries in 1536 many houses resisted and the King's vengeance was ruthless with abbots hanged and buildings torn down. Abbot John Ripley did not resist and surrendered his house on 22 November 1539 and he was rewarded by his abbey being allowed to stand and this is why so much remains to the

Members of the South Pennine Packhorse Trails Trust meet at the old Packhorse Inn on wet and windy Widdop Moor in a valiant effort to keep the old routes open.

present day. Henry also allowed John Ripley to convert the abbey gatehouse into a dwelling and this, now separated from the main abbey by the A65, is one of the finest folk museums we know. The abbey itself is freely open, but there is a small charge for the museum which has a spacious car park. The Abbot's house remained as a private house until 1925 when Basil Harding Butler sold it to Leeds Corporation. On two occasions we spent a whole day at Kirkstall and we still hadn't had enough. We wandered round 18th and 19th-century streets and shops brought here from the Leeds area brick by brick and rebuilt so well that all their atmosphere has journeyed with them. We sat in the Hark to Rover Inn complete with spittoons, flag floors and hand pumps. A look at the prices set the heart pumping — brandy 3d, 4d and 6d, blended whisky 3s 6d a bottle with Glenlivet at 6d, 3d and 2d per glass. What a headache these prices could cause, but never fear because there is an old chemist shop nearby. This displays the once familiar huge bottles of green, yellow, red and blue liquids. This practice dates back to the time of the apothecaries and represents the four basic elements of earth, air, fire and water. An amusing sight is a tobacconist's shop once owned by a man called Haddock, whilst children from four to ninety stand enthralled in front of the collection of old toys and children's books and the museum has so much material that its display is changed frequently and is therefore a good reason to return to the old Gatehouse.

Another fascinating settlement which also lies on the River Aire and the canal is Bingley with the five rise locks being one of the wonders of the canal age and the parish church of All Saints dating back to Saxon times although the present building is Norman. A water bus service runs during the summer along the canal between Bingley and Saltaire, the latter a workers' village built around the mill of Sir Titus Salt, constructed in 1853. He provided library, congregational church, alms houses, hospital and school for his workforce — indeed everything save an ale house! A footpath crosses the river, on the banks of which are a cafe and boathouse where rowing boats are for hire during the summer. On the opposite side of the Aire is Roberts Park from which a cable railway runs up to Shipley Glen which can also be reached by road. The woodlands of the Glen are always a delight, but especially in springtime when it is a mass of bluebells.

One stretch of the Leeds to Liverpool canal which is particularly well known to walkers of the Pennine Way is between Thornton-in-Craven and Gargrave where the route actually follows the towpath. At this point the canal punches its way through the Aire Gap. The route leads through East Marton where there is a bridge by which the A59 crosses the canal. Actually it is two bridges one above the other, with the lower structure dating to the time of the Turnpikes but no longer capable of handling heavy traffic. Below the bridge is a delightful canal basin and also a milestone recording that at this point the canal is $38\frac{1}{2}$ miles from Leeds and 89 miles from Liverpool. There is a mooring point for pleasure craft and one of the areas best pubs — the Cross Keys which serves bar snacks and has an excellent restaurant.

Gargrave is one of our favourite spots. Through it flows both the canal and the River Aire. Above Gargrave the term Airedale is for some reason abandoned in favour of Malhamdale one of the most visited areas in the whole of the Pennines and which

A Victorian Street scene has been faithfully created in the Kirkstall Abbey museum.

is described in chapter seven. Gargrave has been a crossing point over the Pennine via the Aire gap since before recorded time, and it was used extensively by Romans, Saxons, Danes, Normans and indeed is still a vital crossroads. Despite this the village has retained its tranquillity.

Upstream of Bingley is Keighley which claims to be the Pennine Centre but the same claim is made by Saddleworth on the Huddersfield Narrow canal and by Hebden Bridge on the Rochdale.

The Huddersfield Narrow canal is around 20 miles in length and is thus the shortest canal across the Pennines. It is, however, also the most elevated and presented the engineers with phenomenally difficult problems, which taxed even the innovative brains of the Chief Engineer Benjamin Outram and also Thomas Telford himself. To cover the distance a total of 72 locks had to be built an average of more than 3 locks for every mile of navigation. Despite all difficulties it was constructed very quickly following the Act of Parliament in 1794, and was open to traffic in 1811. It linked via the Ashton canal to Manchester and the Mersey on the Lancashire side of the Pennines to Huddersfield and the Calder Navigation and eventually the Humber estuary on the Yorkshire side.

The real engineering feat of the Huddersfield Narrow was the remarkable Standedge Tunnel which is the highest and longest canal tunnel in Britain being 3 miles 135 yards long (4950 metres) and around 645 feet (196 metres) above sea-level. There is no towpath through the tunnel and just as at Foulridge on the Leeds to Liverpool the horses were taken over the moorland whilst the barges were propelled through the cutting by the exhausting process of 'legging'. At the Yorkshire end of the tunnel is a Visitor's Centre but before describing this we must return to the Lancashire end of the tunnel at Saddleworth. We should point out that much of the Saddleworth area was, until the 1974 boundary changes a part of Yorkshire and many still think of themselves as supporters of the White Rose.

Dobcross, Diggle and Delph is not, as might be implied at first glance, a firm of solicitors but three of the moorland villages which make up Saddleworth. Actually there is no actual village of Saddleworth this being an all-embracing term for an area focussed upon Uppermill and also including Denshaw, Greenfield and Grasscroft all reached from the large town of Oldham which we described in our book *Discovering Inland Lancashire*.

Our first introduction to this area was on a dismal evening of sweeping rain and sleet. We were to deliver a lecture on the wild life of Northern England at Uppermill and little did we know at the time that we would eventually be engaged to deliver more than 20 lectures per annum over a period of 12 years! We now know these Pennine moorlands in winter when the snowfalls can be truly frightening: in March when the month not only comes in like the proverbial lion but often goes out the same way — lambing is late in these parts. The winds howl like an Apache from the hills. Indeed this analogy is not far from the mark as a walk up on to the moors with such evocative names as Pots and Pans and Indian Head and which look just like the set of a John Ford western.

We also made a number of radio and television films on the area around the dramatic Dovestones reservoir above Greenfield which holds over 1,000 million gallons of water. Although only completed in 1968 it has, ecologically speaking,

Kirkstall is one of the best preserved of all the Cistercian Abbeys.

settled down very well into an existing sequence of waters including Yeoman Hey, Greenfield and Chew reservoirs which are the highest such waters in England. A look at a map of Saddleworth will reveal many smaller reservoirs which must have affected the flow of water along the River Tame which has its source above Denshaw and then flows westwards to meet the Etherow and Goyt near Stockport the trio then being renamed the Mersey. These constructions must have lowered the water table and hence affected the wildlife. Marsh St Johns wort *Hypericum elodes* and Bog orchid *Hammarbya paludosa* have both disappeared from the area, although there are pressed specimens in the herbarium at Oldham museum.

The changes, however, are not all regrettable. Many reservoirs, including Dovestones, are now highly popular with boaters, windsurfers, anglers and birdwatchers. Even on the coldest days of winter, providing the roads are free from snow there is no shortage of visitors who are provided with toilets and information. Many come to see the mountain or blue hares, although strictly speaking they cannot be regarded as native. The scientific name for the species is *Lepus timidus*, but it is also known as the varying, Arctic, Scottish or Irish hare. In the British Isles it is native to the Highlands of Scotland, the Isle of Man and Ireland, although during the Ice Ages it was found throughout much of England. Around 1880 there were efforts to introduce the species to Derbyshire and the Pennines, but this only seems to have been successful around Saddleworth. It is smaller and stockier than the brown hare *Lepus capensis*, has shorter ears and despite its name of *timidus* does not seem any less wary than its larger cousin. The Arctic hare moults three times each year, another point of contrast to the brown hare and most other British mammals which moult only twice. In summer and autumn the coat is dusky brown, with greyish underfur which is particularly obvious around the flanks. Between early June and mid-September there is what may be described as a 'normal moult' whilst from mid October to early February there is a colour change to white which is an ideal adaptation to life up in the snow where hungry predators lurk. Sometimes in the Saddleworth area this white colour can be a disadvantage as when there is no snow it stands out clearly against dark millstone grit. Finally the animals moult from white

Salt's Mill at Saltaire overlooking the Leeds to Liverpool Canal.

to brown at sometime between mid-February and late May. Some individuals — usually leverets born late in the year do not moult completely and have a piebald appearance. The courtship of the mountain hare is less aggressive than that of the brown hare; the so-called March hare boxing matches apparently play no part in the breeding cycle. The males follow the females at a slow lope, and should he approach too close he is given just one sharp box around the ears. The breeding season usually extends from February to August. Three litters are usual and occasionally there are four with as many as three leverets per litter. There are no records of mountain hares breeding in the year of their birth. On moors with succulent heather they tend to breed earlier and have larger litters. Thus the grouse moors of Scotland are ideal sites, but places like Saddleworth, where there is no active management, are not good for the hares whose population is barely holding its own.

The bird life around Saddleworth is impressive and includes merlin, cuckoo and ring-ousel which is closely related to the blackbird. This disappears as the trees thin out and the thick cover of heather and bilberry is taken over by the ring ousel which is often called the mountain blackbird. Its strident calls echo from the weathered rocks and along the banks of fast-running upland streams which also support dippers. Nightjars once nested in the area although it is many years since they were regular visitors here but golden plover, lapwing, curlew, wheatear and short-eared owl all breed here. Plant species include hard fern, tormentil and bog asphodel, the latter once collected by the mill lasses who boiled the roots to produce a liquid with which they bleached their hair.

Down in the valley of the Tame and its tributaries it is always a pleasure to explore the string of villages which make up Saddleworth, beginning in Uppermill which is the nerve centre of the district. We have often heard visitors refer to Uppermill as Saddleworth which must be annoying to the inhabitants of the other villages even though it is the site of the main Wednesday market, shopping centre, civil hall, council offices and the neat little museum.

The car park at Uppermill is on the site of the Victoria Mill constructed in the 1860s, closing in the 1930s after a life functioning mainly as a cotton spinning mill. The museum,

Boating is popular on the River Aire at Saltaire.

fast developing into one of the north's most interesting tourist attractions, is housed in what was once the mill's gas house. Exhibits provide a comprehensive coverage of the history and natural history of the area. Running alongside the museum is an attractively restored section of the Huddersfield Narrow canal. High Street, the main road through the village was built as part of the Oldham to Standedge Turnpike road which was built around 1790. On the opposite side of the road to the museum is the Alexandra Mill also constructed in the 1860s but this specialised in wool rather than cotton spinning. Its main product was flannel for which the area was justly famed, but in the late 19th century many a Lancashire lassies' shawl had its origins in this part of Tameside. For really excellent views of the area we always enjoy leaving Uppermill via Moorgate and crossing the canal at Spring Gardens. This used to be known by a much more practical name — clogger's knowl — and if the lower block of cottages is examined closely you can see that it was once a public house. The path then crosses the Manchester to Huddersfield railway which was constructed in 1849, but for much of the stroll you are actually on the ancient pre-Roman track towards a ford over the River Tame now overlooked by playing fields. The ancient track was disrupted during the construction of the Huddersfield Narrow canal, but it can be identified once again after crossing Ladcastle Road and ascending steeply onto the eastern slopes of Wharmton. In order to see Uppermill at its best one should follow Ladcastle Road as far as Saddleworth Golf Club. Take a long hard look at the Club House, close your eyes and have a think about life in the good old days. The house used to be called 'The Mountain Ash', after the Rowan tree which still grows in these parts, and was once one of the area's most visited pleasure grounds with swingboats, other amusements and picnic areas plus refreshments; there was also a good supply of home brewed ale on tap. The view below reveals roads, canal and railway squeezed into the valley of the Tame with most of the available spaces utilised as mill sites. We were once told by an old countryman with brains in his head and a wicked twinkle in his eye and who interrupted our conversation on the development of mills in the valley with the words 'When thas finished gawkin' at 'istory med by fo-ak'

Anglers and swans have learned to live together in peace — almost.

he said 'doant fergit to look up at 'ills that God med long afore we was invented'. Lifting the eyes from the villages and the war memorial standing out against the sky can be seen the wind-shaped rocks known locally as Pots and Pans. It used to be said that this was a Druid's altar, but there is no doubt that it is formed only by erosion, and has been formed in a similar manner to the Tors of Dartmoor. The rocks are formed on Kinderscout Grit, a particularly resistant type of millstone grit and therefore in great demand as building stone. The quarries of this area have been worked for centuries, reaching a peak during the period of the Industrial Revolution of the mid 19th century.

Greenfield village took its name from the days when it was just that — a green field in the midst of a stony difficult-to-work land. Until the early 19th century the village did not actually exist although the Chew valley road had been a branch of the Oldham to Standedge road. It is difficult to imagine what this old road was like in the days when there was open country here rather than a complex of domestic and industrial buildings. In the early days there was only a cluster of cottages and the Toll Bar Cottage at Frenches. Towards the end of the 18th century woollen mills were being established, one of the most important being Greenfield Mill situated near Dovestones reservoir and is still working but now as a paper works. As steam took over from water large cotton spinning mills developed at Waterside and Wellington, no doubt influenced by events in Oldham which was becoming one of the world's most important spinning centres. The Greenfield mills drew in such large numbers of workers that terraces of houses were built with indecent haste. Typical of these is a block of what were once back-to-back cottages called Forty Row and which housed the workers of Greenfield Mill. Some greenery remains in the shape of Churchill Playing fields which is the site for the annual Saddleworth Country Fair which is the most important event in the valley.

Dobcross is well known to cinemagoers as it was the location for the filming of Yanks being chosen because it had changed so little since the Second World War. Although it is mainly residential these days it was once one of the most important trading centres in Saddleworth. Look at the village square and you are viewing an area which has changed little, if at all, in the last 200 years. If you want to see what old weavers' cottages were like before the construction of large mills then Dobcross is the place for you, and the church of the Holy Trinity would also have been used by the old weavers. It was constructed in 1788 with the clock tower being added as a result of public subscription in 1843.

Diggle is another traditional industrial area, but unlike Dobcross it has been rather swamped by unimaginative residential developments. Life in Diggle must once have been very isolated, the village stretched out like an old dog at the foot of Broadstone Hill. We wonder what disruption the local folk felt during the construction of the Standedge tunnels as first the canal and then the rail-link were pushed through the Pennines. The labourers employed on these projects lived tough, played hard and must have given the peaceful life of the weavers something of a severe jolt.

Delph on the other hand still has many features associated with weaving including cottages, a wall on which wool was dried and a set of tenter posts on which the yarn was stretched still

Golcar is now quite a large town, but the old village centre is still much
as it was when the handloom weavers were working at full pressure.

exist in a nearby field. Apart from textiles the village also had a reputation for its Delph stone which was quarried nearby in quantity for use in furnaces because of its great resistance to heat. About half a mile to the north west of Delph is the 18th-century church which is now disused. The locals call it Heights church which is a good name for a building sited over 1000 feet (305 metres) above sea level.

Denshaw stands on the northern border of Saddleworth and close to the source of the River Tame. Travel through these moorland areas has never been easy and places such as Denshaw were of vital importance as they stood at crossroads. Five roads meet here leading to Rochdale, Huddersfield, Halifax and Oldham plus the sweeping winding road up and across the moorland. Denshaw is part of the Friarmere area of Saddleworth, but it was previously known by the delightful name of Hilderbrighthope. In Norman times it belonged to the Cistercian monks of Roche Abbey near Sherwood Forest but at the dissolution of this establishment by Henry VIII the area was purchased by Arthur Assheton of Rochdale but by 1551 Denshaw was in the hands of the Gartside family who also hailed from Rochdale. Gartside is still a well known name in the area, as a glance at the local telephone directory will soon prove.

As traffic built up during the Industrial Revolution, turnpike roads were constructed and it was a this time that the Junction Inn was developed. It was built by James Milnes in response to the passing of the Oldham to Ripponden Turnpike in 1795. Later a branch road was constructed to Delph. In 1806 the Act was passed allowing the construction of the Huddersfield to New Hey Turnpike to replace the ancient packhorse route to Rochdale which passed in front of the Junction Inn. In 1807 the Inn had stabling for 40 horses and until the coming of the railway, stage coaches regularly halted here for refreshments and a change of horses on the route from Manchester to Halifax.

To return to the line of the Huddersfield Narrow canal it is best to travel to the Canal and Countryside Centre at the Yorkshire end of the Standedge tunnel. There is a twelve mile circular walk linking the two ends of the tunnel passing over Roman, medieval and packhorse routes as well as

Stoodley Pike is one of the most dramatic monuments on the Pennine range.

a good example of the work of Blind Jack of Knaresborough. A leaflet describing the circular walk can be purchased from the Information Centres at Tunnel End and at Brownhill. The Standedge guide provides even more detail describing the trans-Pennine communication systems over the past 2,000 years. For those who prefer level rather than hill walks there is a seven mile long path from Tunnel End at Marsden to the centre of Huddersfield which passes old weavers' cottages, snug little hamlets and impressive textile mills set below the canal in the valley bottom. At various points along the canal are interpretive boards. The Pennine Way passes close to Marsden and we once met a hardy couple who had diverted from the main route to walk the canal towpath and also Rapes Highway one of the finest packhorse routes in the area. They were the perfect example of Pennine lovers as opposed to those who merely walk with their heads down. What joys await Pennine strollers who take their time and enjoy the history and natural history of the area.

Along the canal are a number of picnic sites and car parks whilst at Golcar the village of weavers' cottages has survived being swamped by modern buildings. The history of the area is well told in the Colne Valley Museum housed in a group of weavers' cottages built about 1840 at the top of a narrow cobbled lane. It is open from 2pm to 5pm at weekends and on public holidays. The museum sells a leaflet describing a twelve mile circular walk around the Upper Colne valley.

The initiative to preserve the canal gathered momentum throughout the 1980s and looks like continuing into the 1990s the lead being taken by the Huddersfield Canal Society. The Kirklees Council have also played their part in restoring the canal. Thus in the last twenty years great strides have been made in the restoration of all three trans-Pennine canals.

The Rochdale Canal began its life under the guidance of none other than John Rennie, the construction being authorized in 1794. Its 32 mile length runs from Manchester to Sowerby Bridge from which it joined the River Calder-Hebble navigation. Rennie did not, however, take much part in the down-to-the-earth planning and construction of the cut — this was done by William Jessop. By 1804 the Rochdale was open and provided the first water route across the Pennines and

The Arctic Hare: Eating snow in winter when liquid water is not available, and also searching for grass beneath the snow.

linking Lancashire with Yorkshire. It is therefore fitting that it should pass through Todmorden as its town hall straddles the old county boundary. In terms of tonnage of cargo carried this was the most successful of the trans-Pennine canals. One of the first carriers to operate was Thomas Carver of Halifax who in 1808 ran his business from Dale Street in Manchester, whilst Pickfords were soon in competition by operating a fleet of fly boats. These fly boats were the canal equivalents of our data post or red star delivery service. They were actually narrowboats constructed to slightly smaller dimensions and capable of carrying around 20 tons but with a draught of only 2 feet 6 inches. There was a night service which could cover the distance between Manchester and Littleborough in nine hours whilst a further three hours brought the boat to its moorings in Todmorden. Every time a lock is operated it loses water and the Rochdale required 92 of these structures; thus it needed a number of feeder reservoirs near the summit area. These were at White Holme, Lighthazzles, Warland, Blackstone Edge, Chelburn, Littleborough and Hollingworth Lake. The latter which we fully described in our volume on *Inland Lancashire* was soon in use as a leisure area by the mill workers and became affectionately known as 'weivers' seaport'. It is now the focus of a substantial Country Park. From the Hollingworth area the canal climbs to its summit around Littleborough and then down to Todmorden. The line of the cut is followed by the road between Rochdale and Todmorden and passes the restored toll house at Steanor Bottom. The minor road signed Lumbutts is worth following and which first crosses the canal and then climbs steeply to the summit of a hill from which there are panoramic views over Todmorden and the Upper Calder Valley. Nearby is a spacious old inn called The Shepherds Rest and by the side of the car park is an old stable block with horses still in residence and we watched them being groomed, walked out and exercised. From the inn the road descends steeply into Lumbutts which is nothing more than a hamlet clustered around a tower. This once provided power to a spinning mill which contained three overshot waterwheels fed from a complicated series of dams and syphons receiving their water from Black Clough. In 1991 the complex was converted into an activity centre with the tower used by trainee climbers, the mill dams for watersports but with areas set aside for wildlife and hikes into the hills organised and supervised. Self-catering accommodation for up to 24 visitors is provided in lockable well furnished, single, double and small dormitory bedrooms all with washrooms and some with en suite facilities. Special accommodation for the disabled is available on the main level with a bedroom suite for supporting staff. Outdoor equipment may be hired and there are drying areas and other spaces suitable for lectures. This is set to expand during the 1990s and details are available by ringing 0706 814536.

From Lumbutts the road ascends past what was once a complex of mill workers' houses some of which have been beautifully renovated, brightly painted and garlanded with sweet smelling flowers during the warmer months of the year. Half way up the hill is the *Top Brink Inn* an old establishment once known as *The Dog and Partridge*. 'Beyond the Brink' so to speak is a footpath leading to one of the

Skaters enjoying the frozen water of Hollingworth lake in the 1890s.

most interesting monuments in the Pennines — Stoodley Pike. This was constructed during a period of euphoria when the abdication of Napoleon in 1814 brought the Peace of Ghent. We wonder what folk who had been under threat for most of their lives felt when the emperor went back on his word and was defeated at Waterloo by Wellington in 1815. The monument had to be restored in 1856 after being struck by lightening. The £812 required for its construction was raised by public subscription and the 120 foot high (36.5 metres) monument can be entered from the north side and mounted by a stone staircase to a balcony about 40 feet (12 metres). The view from this is magnificent and the footpath snaking down to Mankinholes can be clearly seen.

Mankinholes is of great antiquity and situated in the area of Langfield which was one of the 'Berewics' belonging to the manor of Wakefield. Mentioned in Domesday it was given during the early days of Norman rule to the Earl of Warren from whom it passed into the hands of the Hammerton. So it remained until Sir Richard Hammerton made a crucial error in opposing the will of Henry VIII who was determined to dissolve the monasteries. This led in 1537 to a northern-based rebellion known as the Pilgrimage of Grace, which from its onset was doomed to failure. Many monks and other leaders were executed and Sir Richard Hammerton lost both his head and his lands which were forfeited to the crown. Religion of a contentious and challenging nature seems to have been a feature of Mankinholes — perhaps because of its isolation — and in 1653 the teachings of George Fox who founded the Quakers found a warm welcome on this Pennine hillside. The house of Joshua Laycock at Bottom-of-the-town became a focus for quaker activities and in 1667 a burial ground was consecrated. The burial ground still remains in the village at 'Tenter Croft' which was rented for 'two pennyworth of silver for a period of 900 years'. As the Industrial Revolution gathered pace the Quakers moved their meeting house nearer to Todmorden but perhaps their decision was influenced by a relaxation of the laws insisting on strict adherence to the established church. Once the Quakers had gone Mankinholes was left without a religious house of any sort, and so remained until John Wesley arrived in the Todmorden area and set the hearts and souls of local folk on fire with the love of God. Wesley first came to these breezy hills in 1743 and in 1753 he returned to preach in General Wood in Walsden whilst it was the home of James Rhodes. In his diary Wesley records that he had time for his hosts to mend his clothes and make him a new shirt. His preachings obviously went home with chapels springing up throughout the area and around 1815 one was built at Mankinholes and a school opened at the same time its master being William Bayes of Lumbutts.

The next settlement along the Rochdale Canal and which also lies on the River Calder is Hebden Bridge and beyond this is Sowerby Bridge both of which are described in the next chapter.

CHAPTER 5

The Calderdale Way

Because it crosses the Pennine Way and is only 50 miles around, the Calderdale Way is often underated as a long distance footpath. There are, however, many linking footpaths which can double its length and we once spent a whole week on the route and there were still many areas left unexplored. Since then we have had several weeks with boots and cameras, in all weathers and with a variety of knowledgeable and interested companions. The well marked way originated in 1973 and as a result of cooperation between Civic Societies, Conservation groups, and others a map of the route was produced. The essential finance was found by the Countryside Commission and the West Yorkshire County Council; the Way was opened on 21st October 1978 and was the first 'Recreational Path' in the country. The publicity it generated brought visitors into the area and also acted as a focus for local interest, thus stimulating new projects along the valley and on the banks of the canals described in the last chapter. For those who prefer to discover the Pennines by strolling rather than by lung-bursting walks there are several towns and villages which provide interest, inns and are ideal centres for a day's walking or driving. Included are Todmorden, Hebden Bridge and Heptonstall, Mytholmroyd and Cragg Vale, Sowerby Bridge, Halifax, Brighouse and Rastrick of brass band fame, and Ripponden which is situated close to the M62 motorway. Thus Ripponden is an ideal gateway into the Calder Valley.

Also close to the M62 is Elland which has a pretty canal basin and a lovely little medieval bridge. Above the settlement the motorway runs along Scammonden Dam and then through the biggest motorway cutting in Europe at Dean Head. There is a bridge with a 410 foot (125 metre) span and just a little to the west of this at Windy Hill the Pennine Way crosses the M62 by means of a narrow bridge.

Todmorden has been described as an ugly town with a split personality. This is a half-true observation, a rumour spread by those who have read a little, travelled straight through poor old 'Tod' and not had the sense to stop. It is true that it is a typical Pennine town, built of dark millstone grit made even darker by the fumes of the Industrial Revolution. It does have a split personality as the Calder running beneath the town hall is the old boundary between Lancashire and Yorkshire although lads born in the town are all accepted as true-born tykes and therefore eligible to play cricket for Yorkshire. Not to stop in the town is an insult as the outdoor market is one of the busiest in the Pennines and overlooked by a towering railway viaduct bringing the country to the town every Wednesday, Friday and Saturday. For travellers wanting to take back a memory of the area or that special gift for a friend should choose Thursday when there is a bric-a-brac market. Decorating our study are several horse brasses, a couple of shuttles from an old cotton mill and a battered old packhorse bell forged in Wigan which specialised in their production. The bells were essential along the busy but narrow packhorse routes when visibility was reduced by driving rain and mist still a feature of the surrounding moorlands. The Tourist Information Centre on the main street near the town hall is large and the staff friendly and knowledgable.

Todmorden market can be misleading since the town did not grow up around the market but rather developed to serve the needs of a rapidly expanding industrial area. Even the town hall is a product of the wealth created by cotton. It was built by the three Fielden brothers, who did so much to bring much needed reform into factory practices of the time, and when it opened on 25 April 1875 it had cost £54,000 — a staggering sum at that time. The brothers thought it a fitting memorial to their father and their uncles who founded their thriving business and the people of Todmorden are rightly proud of it. The building is constructed in the classical style with graceful pillars dominating the front. There are three niches over the front which are empty but some have suggested that the brothers may have intended to insert their own statues in the spaces and then thought better of it. A pair of binoculars are useful if focused on the upper frieze which tells the history of the town; Todmorden is placed in its geographical position in one carving with others reflecting its agricultural heritage and the story of the cotton industry on a third.

Hebden Bridge lies at the junction of the River Calder with its tributary the Hebden. It is often described as an industrial small town and much underated because of it. We have often read that Heptonstall is the historic settlement overlooking the more vulgar town. What a shame not to visit and enjoy Hebden Bridge which buzzes with tourists during the Thursday market day and on summer weekends when most shops stay open and the Information Centre keeps everyone up to date with events.

If you like old bridges, historic inns, canal cruises and nostalgic old railway stations then this is the place for you. Any tour of the town should begin at the old bridge because the town grew up naturally around it. There was certainly a wooden bridge over the Hebden in 1477 and the need for a stout stone structure on the route from Heptonstall to Halifax was essential. In 1508 John Greenwood of Wadsworth left the then substantial sum of 6 shillings and 8 pence (34 pence) to the priest at Heptonstall and half this sum 'to the fabric of "Hepton" Bridge.' In the same year William Mergatroyd left 6s 8d and in 1510 Richard Naylor left the same sum. Among the currency in use at this period was the noble worth 6s 8d (33 pence) and the mark worth 13s 4d (66 pence). One noble plus one mark made up one pound.

Once a stone bridge was erected an area of permanence was created around it and acted as a focal point for inns and a blacksmith's forge which all catered for the packhorse trade. There was already a mill on the river which used water power to drive the wheel. This ground the corn for Heptonstall which was high up on the hillside. Later a mill chimney was erected as steam power came into use around 1820. Both water wheel and steam were still in partial use until the 1950s since which time the three storey building has been put to use as a craft centre, shop and restaurant.

Near the bridge is the Hole-in-the-Wall on the Heptonstall side and, although it was rebuilt about 100 years ago and some buildings opposite were demolished; the ancient cobbled packhorse track leading steeply up from the bridge to Heptonstall is still in use today. The splendid White Lion dated 1657 is one of Hebden Bridge's few old houses and was probably constructed on the site of a wooden building. Up until the late 18th century it was known as 'Kings Farm' as it had been the working home of Susan and James King during the late 17th century. As the turnpike roads were pushed through the valley during the late 18th and early 19th century the White Lion was converted to an inn and was a vital stop on the Rochdale to Halifax route, a period remembered by the plaque over the doorway. At this time a new bridge over the Calder was built and this carries traffic today, whilst the old Hebden Bridge is only used by pedestrians.

Although the Rochdale Canal ceased to carry goods in 1939 it has now been restored and there are regular tourist trips along the cut from the centre of the town. One important archeological feature is the Black Pit aqueduct which carries the canal over the River Calder.

The railway at Hebden Bridge also has much to offer the historian as the station has retained many 19th-century features including the wooden notices and signs plus the cast iron canopy so typical of early stations. Looking at the platforms it seems as if they had been built on sandstone blocks — in fact the blocks were, until 1977 the platform itself and special blocks had to be provided to allow the infirm to climb down from the train to the platform which was lately raised. The Calder Valley line was one of the earliest to be built and George Stephenson was the engineer who followed through the plans approved by an Act of Parliament in 1836. The line ran from Manchester to Normanton near Wakefield where it connected with the line linking Leeds and Derby. The Calder Valley line opened on 1st March 1841, a remarkable achievement when it is realised that the Summit Tunnel had to be punched through 2885 yards (879 metres) of solid rock and the structure was, at the time of its construction, the longest tunnel in the world. The whole line was 60 miles long and the journey was at first scheduled to take only three hours which must have seemed miraculous to those used to travelling along turnpike or canal. First class passengers were guaranteed a roof over their head, a seat and a proper window. Second class passengers were denied glass in the window whilst third class travellers had to stand up in an uncovered wagon. Even the latter was an improvement on

Heptonstall churches — ancient and modern.

the road coaches and it is no wonder that pleasure excursions by train soon became popular.

Although the rail link is still open most visitors these days arrive by car and an increasing number visit Childhood Reflections which has a display of dolls, toys and miniatures.

At Easter 1992 the museum moved to Walkley's Clogg Mill further along the Rochdale Canal (see p. 74). Another recent feature seems to be a little incongruous but is guaranteed to provide an excited jolt is the Hebden Crypt described as a museum of myths, legend and horror. This display which opened in 1990 features Sweeny Todd, Dracula and King Arthur's magic sword. All this and more from a museum whose doors creak open each day from 10.30 am to 4 pm except Mondays when it is closed.

The industry of Hebden Bridge is also of interest to the historian and the Nutclough works is of particular interest; from 1873 to 1919 Nutclough mill was the basis of a Fustian Manufacturing Society which was one of the first 'producer cooperatives'. Its members were able to combine their funds and operate from luxurious premises. Fustian was made first from flax and later from cotton being dyed in a dark colour and having a short pile or nap. Such material was ideal for the manufacture of blankets. The manufacturers such as Robert Halstead, Joseph Greenwood and Joseph Craven became famous for providing a compromise between socialism and capitalism. All the leaders of this movement were enlightened in the way they treated their workers and Robert Halstead was one of the leading lights in setting up the Workers Educational Association (WEA), for whom we lectured for many years.

Based at Hebden Bridge three fascinating places should be visited — Heptonstall, Hardcastle Craggs and Automobilia. The modern visitor to Heptonstall can be excused for thinking that it developed as an offshoot of Hebden Bridge. In fact Heptonstall developed much earlier and made its living from handloom weaving of wool which was then taken down from the hillside by packhorse, over the Hebden Bridge and on to the main market at Halifax. A very sensible Conservation Order protects the village and a steep descent of the main street passes old dairy farms, colourful cottages, the old village pump, two churches, an assortment of inns with cobbled yards and the old cloth hall now a private residence. At the bottom of the street is a spacious car park close to cafes, toilets and an excellent fish and chip shop and from it here is a sign to the museum. This is situated in the old Grammar School endowed in 1642 by the Revd Charles Greenwood who was

The clogger has long been a part of South Pennine life.

also the Lord of the Manor of Heptonstall. The school, which was rebuilt in 1771, had an excellent reputation and only closed in 1898 then being considered to be too small. This reason for closure is still being used a century later; up until 1954 the building was a sub-branch of the Yorkshire Penny Bank and since then it has been a small but very informative museum. The Heptonstall Grammar School Museum has several times been threatened with closure — perhaps they should increase the small admission charge — and it would be a disaster if ever it failed to reflect the history of the town. The museum opens at weekends between 1 p.m. and 5 p.m. with an extension of a further hour between April and September. At Easter and between May and August it also opens on weekdays except Tuesdays from 11 am to 4 pm. The old school is remembered in a display including the master's high desk surrounded by the pupils' benches with quill pens, ink wells and even the master's spectacles. Other exhibitions depict the art of the wheelwright, a complete 18th-century kitchen and a large collection of archive photographs. There is also a collection of maces which were once wielded by the Heptonstall Prosecution Society which kept the peace between 1816 and 1909. If law-keepers are recognised here then so is a law breaker. David Hartley was a counterfeit coiner who made illegal money by clipping pieces of silver from coins and then melting these down to produce new money. 'King David' and his crew worked in Cragg Vale a wooded valley outside the village and were much feared until their leader was arrested. His fate is entered in the church records for 1st May 1770 and which reads 'David Hartley of Bell House in the township of Erringden, hanged by the neck near York for unlawfully stamping and clipping the public coin.' Despite his evil deeds David was laid to rest in the churchyard which is shared by two churches. A chapel was built at Heptonstall in 1256 and dedicated to St Thomas à Becket but this was devastated by a storm in 1847. In an age not noted for its sentimentality the villagers were allowed to leave the shell and build a new church dedicated to St Thomas the Apostle in 1850. The clock from the old church which was made at Sowerby Bridge in 1809 was transferred to the new tower in 1854. The view of the new church through the ruins of the old is spectacularly haunting, but John Wesley who preached a great deal in Calderdale was much less complimentary. He wrote 'I preached in Heptonstall church, the ugliest church I know.'

Perhaps his view inspired Wesley's followers to build a Methodist chapel in 1764 and Wesley was the first to preach in

The canal at Sowerby Bridge with the Wainhouse tower in the background.

the attractive octagonal building. It has been used for worship ever since and is the oldest Methodist chapel in the world still in use. Rudyard Kipling's maternal grandfather was minister here and it is inferred rather than positively proved that the writer spent some time living with him and roving the moorlands whilst his parents were away in India. There is written evidence to support this view as Kipling included in one of his Indian stories in which he describes similarities between a Himalayan hillside and the Pennines 'Moors an' moors an' moors, wi' never a tree for shelter, an' grey houses wi' flagstone rooves, and peewits cryin', and a windhover goin' too and fro just like these kites.' The lapwing which Kipling called the peewit and the kestral are still common on the Pennines and seem to prove that the writer knew this area. If this was the case then he must have known Hardcastle Craggs, one of our favourite walks and one of the best places in the Pennines both for its flora and fauna. Red squirrels are still found here among the pines and larches and these coniferous areas are also popular with wood ants whose huge nests are becoming increasingly common. The ants' nests attract both jays and green woodpeckers which we have seen dancing up and down on the heaps of pine needles much to the annoyance of the ants. This behaviour is called anting and it has been proved that the angry ants spray formic acid at the birds and this kills the lice which are trapped among the feathers. This is nature's own aerosol spray and is ozone friendly.

There are car parks close to the Craggs near Heptonstall and the area is also well signed from Hebden Bridge off the road to Keighley. From this there is a steep descent through a tapestry of trees leading into a valley cut by Hebden Water. Hardcastle Craggs gets its name from the large piles of angular rocks, eroded by wind, ice and water which line the valley sides. Dippers bob up and down on the stones in the water and kingfisher breed close to the now disused Gibson's Mill and flash under the old tollbridge. This still bears a legible price list showing that a sheep could be taken across for a half-penny, but a horse and trap had to pay two pence. A National Trust Nature Trail leads from the car park for which a modest fee is charged to Slurring Rock, a name derived from the sound made by generations of children sliding down the rock in iron-shod clogs.

We have enjoyed many a car drive around this area, but for those in search of an unusual drive then the hire of an old Austin and a 1930s picnic hamper complete with a wind-up gramophone is to be recommended. All this and more can be enjoyed by visiting Automobilia Motor Museum on Billy Lane, Old Town at Wadsworth above Hebden Bridge. The museum of old cars, motor cycles and garage equipment, is open between April to September from Tuesday to Sunday and Bank Holidays from 12 noon to 6 pm. In winter it only opens during weekends from 12 to 6 pm. The major difference between this and other motor museums is that some of the Austin sevens can actually be hired for a day, complete with picnic and gramophone.

The local moorlands were more difficult to explore in the days of the bad old coiners and the good old Wesley. Mytholmroyd was well known to both and in more recent times to Ted Hughes, born in the village and who became Poet Laureate. No wonder he wrote so well about rivers. Mytholmroyd and the nearby Cragg Vale were coiners' country and here worked King David Hartley with his associates

Matthew Normanton and Thomas Spencer who were also hanged, but Isaac Hartley was acquitted because of lack of evidence and died an old man taking his dark secrets to his grave. Some of their hiding places have come to light with Keelham, New House and Bell House still standing in Cragg Vale. John Wesley preached many times in the valley especially at Hoo Hall which stands on private land. Here there was an ancient chestnut tree beneath which Wesley preached but it was so decayed in the 1980s that it had to be felled, but was replaced by another to celebrate the John Wesley festival which took place in Calderdale in 1984.

In these damp valleys full of mills the local workers relied upon well made clogs. Between Mytholmroyd and Hebden Bridge, the old craft of clog making is still practiced at Clog Sole Mill. This is a unique combination of a profit-making clog shop, museum of old machinery plus a rather fine little restaurant. There are two car parks and Walkley's Clogg Mill is open throughout the year including weekends and Bank holidays and entry is free. After a disastrous fire the museum was restored during 1991. Nearby there is also a pottery focused on the old Mytholmroyd fire station which has developed a reputation for producing collectors' items.

If you fancy mumming for pace eggs or a good dose of Passion pudding then Mytholmroyd and the nearby hamlets of Midgley and Luddenden are well worth a visit. To make Passion pudding the leaves of a plant called bistort were collected and boiled with nettles and oats and then fried using a little fat. They take their passion seriously in Mytholmroyd and district and they award a silver cup to the best Easter Dock pudding. It was at Midgley that another Easter custom once widespread in old England was written down and has survived. The old Mummers Pace Egg Play is still performed with great fun and energy by the pupils of Mytholmroyd High School. The word Pace derives as does the Passion of Christ from 'pasch' meaning Easter and at the end of the play the actors were often rewarded by a feast of eggs. The play is just an excuse for an impromptu jaunt with ad-libbing not only accepted but expected and just so long as good triumphed over evil all was well. The essential characters are King George of England, the Dragon slayer, the King of Egypt, the Doctor and Toss Pot. Luddenden's pub is the

The Piece Hall at Halifax — one of the finest buildings along the Pennines and a reminder of its industrial history.

Lord Nelson and it was here that Branwell Brontë stayed when he worked on the local railway as a clerk, until he was sacked for drunkeness.

Sowerby Bridge, like Hebden Bridge, developed around a vital crossing point of the Calder. All the signs are that the

1990s is going to be the decade of Sowerby, as a much more enlightened attitude to tourism takes hold. The local council even filled in one section of a canal, but without disrupting the vital junction of the Rochdale Canal with the Calder and Hebble navigation which itself joins first the Aire and Calder navigation and then the River Ouse to the Humber estuary and the sea. Now that the tourism potential is being realised there are suggestions to reinstate the filled in stretch of canal, but raising the capital is likely to be a problem. The wharf at Sowerby is always full of boats, many of which are for hire whilst the Moorings Hotel produced from an old warehouse serves a variety of bar snacks and meals in an area overlooking the canal. The view along the canal reveals a backdrop formed by Wainhouse Tower an elaborate folly to the west of Halifax its upper viewing platform reached via 403 steps although it is only occasionally open to the public. Built in 1871 it was meant as a chimney to serve a dye-works but the 270 foot octagonal stone chimney was never actually used.

Sowerby Bridge became world famous from 1865 onwards when Joseph Pollit and Eustace Wigzell produced high quality steam engines. Some of the workers had so much overtime that they were able to purchase good houses on Myrtle Row and Tuel Lane which became known locally as Overtime Row. At Longridge among the foothills of the Bowland Fells on the fringes of the Pennines a collection of cottages are known as Club Row. These were built by cotton operatives who 'clubbed' together to produce one house. They then drew lots to decide who should move in and then all the workers combined to produce additional houses until at last all were living in 'Club Row'.

Halifax is dovetailed into the Pennine foothills close to the Hebble brook which rises on the steep slopes which surround the town. It began to prosper as it was the focus of the wool market and its spectacular Piece Hall which was built in 1779 has 315 rooms set around a quadrangle. Here cloth weavers exhibited their lengths of cloth which were known as pieces. This is one of the finest buildings in Yorkshire which has been restored and still is in use, but now occupied by bookshops, cafes, second hand stores, drapers, jewellers and a variety

Ilkley Moor, with or without your hat is a breezy place on the fringes of the Pennines.

of other establishments. The Information Centre is situated here and the whole area bounces with activity on Saturdays and Sundays when an impromptu market is in full swing. Halifax was one of the few towns in England which executed criminals using a gruesome looking guillotine which has now been restored and stands in the well named Gibbet Street. No wonder there was an old saying 'From Hull, Hell and Halifax, good Lord deliver us'. Execution was the punishment for stealing cloth valued at more than 13½d (5½ pence) and this was last exacted in 1650 by which time 50 heads had been severed.

Brighouse is another typical textile town but it also has a fine market, an excellent park at Wellholme and is surrounded by delightful countryside and woodland. The canal is now devoted to pleasure boats and fishing, with local anglers often having to share their sandwiches with the persistent mute swans. There is a local legend which suggests that Robin Hood is buried at Kirklees near Clifton. At this time Brighouse was nothing more than a country hamlet but then came the Industrial Revolution, and the settlement lacked adequate communications. In 1779 John Smeaton canalised the River Calder and in 1834 a new route was cut completely independent of the meandering river. Eventually turnpikes improved communications still further and then came the Manchester to Leeds railway which ensured an easy market for Brighouse cloth. The town has produced its share of remarkable people including John Bateman and Mrs Sunderland who became known as the 'Yorkshire Nightingale'. Bateman was one of the finest civil engineers of the 19th century who specialised in the construction of dams. He was never short of work as industrial towns developed and became ever more thirsty. Many of his works are still evident around the Pennines including Widdop above Colne, and Ogden reservoir above Halifax. John Bateman also enjoyed travel and he built dams in India, Turkey and Argentina.

Mrs Sunderland was a Brighouse lass whose voice was said to be a joy although she made her reputation in Sunderland from which she took her name. Queen Victoria loved her voice and called her the 'Yorkshire Nightingale'. Although the songstress has long been forgotten the town still has a reputation for good music and the Brighouse and Rastrick is one of the finest brass bands in the country.

Ripponden is best explored by leaving the M62 via junction 22 and following the Ryburn valley. This narrow valley was crossed by Daniel Defoe in the 17th century as he battled his way from Rochdale to Huddersfield. Despite the fact that this is the narrowest part of the Pennines the weather can be horrendous and travel in winter can be a problem. The damp climate of the Pennines, however, was perfect for the weaving of textiles and the villages along the Ryeburn valley produced the cloth for the uniforms of the British Navy. In Ripponden the Pennine Farm Museum records the history of the valley having been set up in a converted barn by the Ryeburn Civic Trust in 1975 which was European Heritage year. The village itself is an ideal centre for several circular walks and at its heart is a bridge a mill and a church. There was a Roman ford here but a bridge of wood and stone was in existence by 1313 and in 1533 William Firth gave 7 shillings and 6 pence (37½ pence) towards the building of a more substantial span of stone. This was destroyed by a flood in 1722 when the present bridge was constructed. The road to the bridge may be Roman, but is most probably medieval in origin.

Initially Ripponden had no church and the locals had to trek to Elland; in 1464 St Bartholomew's was built but the present building is the fourth on the site and was dedicated in 1870. In the churchyard is the grave of Sam Hill who in the 18th century organised local weavers into groups working under one roof and thus initiating the factory system in the Calder Valley and having a profound effect far beyond its borders. Between 1706 and 1759 he exported top quality worsteds all over Europe, making full use of the Piece Hall at Halifax. Ripponden is typical of a Pennine settlement being a combination of industry and history plus additional rewards for those who are prepared to walk. Although it is not so well known as the one at Blackstone Edge the stretch of so-called Roman road between Ripponden and Rastrick is still well preserved and worth a close look. Within range of Ripponden are other attractive villages including Rishworth, Barkisland, Hubberton Green, Lumb, Soyland and Mill Bank which itself has been declared a conservation area. At Ringstone Edge there is the site of a Neolithic settlement and the remnant of a stone circle. This proves that this area of the Pennines has been settled for more than five thousand years.

CHAPTER 6

The Aire Gap, Keighley and the Worth Valley

Along the Pennine chain there are two main gaps, one along the valley of the River Aire and the other sliced by the South Tyne. Standing astride the Aire and close to its tributary, the Worth, is Keighley (pronounced Keith-ly) whose guide describes it as the Pennine Town. A settlement here was recorded in the Domesday survey of 1086 and was then called Chichelai and probably developed because of the presence of the River Worth which runs down from Haworth to join the Aire. Keighley does lie close to the Pennine Way and some of the surrounding hills, especially the famous Ilkley Moor, are very popular with walkers. During the Industrial Revolution Keighley developed rapidly and specialised in textiles and also in the machinery which drove mills all over the world. In the mid 20th century it attracted large numbers of immigrants from all over the world and thus it is a fine place to eat with a great variety of restaurants; competition between these ensures competitive prices. It is also a good town for holiday makers to buy a distinctive Pennine present and there are a number of mills which have their own attached shops. Historic buildings are few and far between but East Riddlesden Hall and Cliffe Castle Museum are both worth an extended visit.

East Riddlesden dates mainly to the 17th century, but also has a monastic fish pond and a barn, both pre-15th century. There is evidence to prove that the site was occupied from at least AD 960 when Waltheof the Saxon Earl of Northumbria was the owner and by the time of the Norman conquest this, and many other manors, was in the hands of his grandson Gospatric the Lord of Bingley. After 1066 most Saxons were stripped of their lands, but the old lords of Bingley were lucky and their lands were only absorbed by the Normans as a result of a marriage entered into willingly, when an heiress was joined to Simon de Montalt. He was the eldest son of William FitzHugh FitzWilliam a very powerful Norman with much influence in the North of England. In 1402 East Riddlesden passed once more by marriage on the distaff side to the Paslew family who were very influential in the area around Bingley at this time, but the Riddlesden branch did not seem as energetic as other members of the family. When Ellen Paslew married Robert Rishworth things did not improve and worse was to follow during the stewardship of the Mergatroyd family and there is a local legend that the River Aire changed its course in the 17th century to avoid passing too close to the family. James Murgatroyd made a massive fortune from his Halifax based woollen business and it was he who spent money constructing the fine Jacobean building around the old fish pond, and to do this much of the Tudor half-timbered building was demolished. Murgatroyds and trouble were inseperable and James' three sons were all fined heavily for their brutish behaviour. This led inevitably to bankruptcy, but the family were immortalised in the Gilbert and Sullivan opera 'Rudigore'. W. S. Gilbert who wrote the libretto often stayed at East Riddlesden and must have been aware of their reputation. The family fortunes were only restored when Margaret Murgatroyd married Nicholas Starkie of Huntroyd which is between Burnley and Whalley around 1688. By 1708 the Starkies had restored East Riddlesden but by early in the 19th century they had also run out of male heirs and the two daughters both married Sussex landowners; during the next 120 years the grand old hall declined gradually into a decaying farmhouse. In 1905 the Starkie wing was so ruinous that it had to be pulled down and all that remains today are the mews containing hatches in which the birds of prey were kept. Relief only came in 1933 when the two Brigg brothers bought East Riddlesden and gave it to the National Trust in the following year. Gradually the house was restored and furnished but exciting progress has been made since 1982 and East Riddlesden is without doubt Airedale's most historic hall, and well worth the entry fee. Visitors should not forget to look at the two barns, the larger of the two dating to around 1650. The roof timbering looks very church-like and this may not be an accident as James Mergatroyd is said to have brought some stone from Bolton Priory in Wharfedale and from Kirkstall Abbey further down the Aire to repair the barn. Inside the main hall there is a book and souvenir shop and there is a cafe which sells home made scones and cakes.

Keighley Station is shared by British Rail and the Worth Valley Railway.

A much more modern, but equally fascinating, museum is at Cliffe Castle which was built by a Victorian industrialist specialising in the production of worsted. Here is Keighley's art gallery, museum of local industry, including a clogger's shop, a display of natural history and our favourite which is a collection of minerals some of which are illuminated by ultra-violet light. The gardens are a delight especially in the summer, with flowers surrounding a number of aviaries full of colourful birds. There is a collection of labelled trees, a childrens' play area, and a cafe situated in what was once a conservatory.

Keighley is an ideal centre from which to explore the Worth valley and what better way to do this than by steam train.

The Keighley and Worth Valley Railway has had its share of ups and downs since it opened amid great scenes of excitement on 13 April 1867. It was built as a branch line for the inhabitants of the Worth Valley, and stations were provided at Ingrow, Oakworth, Haworth and Oxenhope. The original plan was to run the single track line through to Hebden Bridge. The scheme, however, proved far too ambitious and it had to stop short at Oxenhope on the edge of the moors. Right up to the time when it closed to passengers on December 30 1961 the Worth Valley railway had carried around 130,000 passengers a year. Naturally when the Beeching Axe fell it brought a wave of protest, but all the noise fell on deaf ears. It was left to the Keighley and Worth Valley Railway Preservation Society to save the line, gather together a rolling stock of steam and diesel locomotives and renovate the stations. This is now an increasingly important tourist attraction — and it deserves all the praise which has been heaped upon it since it was ready for an independent existence in June 1968. The staff are fitted with neat uniforms, their badges and shoes gleam, the ticket office shines with polish produced by a little brasso and a lot of elbow grease. This railway has been used as the setting for many films and television series including 'Yanks', 'The Railway Children', 'The Adventures of Sherlock Holmes' and 'A Woman of Substance.'

We began our journey at Keighley on Platform Four which the Society leases from British Rail. Fortified by a hot chocolate we browsed among the magazines and cards for sale in the old fashioned kiosk. This is reminiscent of the time when the station was built in 1883 to replace the original building which was beyond the bridge to the north. Soon we were comfortably settled in a carriage and on our way up the steep incline towards Haworth. The joy of this line is that you can break your journey anywhere you like and there are some super walks from each and every station. Our first stop was Oakworth. This has no cafe or gift shop and commercialism is reduced to a minimum. It is the society's masterpiece and they have restored the station to the days of its glory at the turn of the century. We found no electricity here — everything was lit by gas and on a chilly windy day we found a blazing fire in the grate. Advertisements relating to the steam period cover the walls and surrounding fence. Milk churns and assorted luggage lie about on the platform as if waiting for the next train. On the wall is an advertisement for a cheap trip from Blackburn to London running from October 1901 to April 1902. The train went into St Pancras and we are told that most trains were heated by steam but if this was not available then foot warmers were provided free, but on all trains blankets and pillows were always available for hire. Inside the ticket office is a token machine

Children's excursions are a popular feature of the Worth Valley line which was used as the set for the film called "The Railway Children."

which was vital in the days when telephone systems were not in regular use. The Worth Valley Railway still uses the system. A train on the line deposits its tally and this is not removed until it returns and the line is clear. Two trains on the same line is therefore impossible. The gardens at Oakworth are so colourful that we were not surprised to learn that the station has won many awards. The next stop up the line is Haworth.

From here it is a delight to stroll up the steep village street to the Parsonage, home of the Brontë family from the 1820s to the 1850s. Forget the stories of how miserable the Brontës found the local countryside. Nobody could write such beautiful prose and be sad all the time. From the parsonage footpaths lead over Penistone Hill to the Brontë waterfalls and Top Withens. This is *Jane Eyre* and *Wuthering Heights* country. We were a little sad ourselves when the time came to return to the train but this is always enjoyable. We looked at the engine sheds and then rejoined the train for the next stop up the line which is the terminus at Oxenhope where once again the Society has worked wonders. A carriage has been converted into a cafe, there is another well stocked shop designed to excite the railway enthusiast, and also an extensive car park. Travellers on the railway are allowed free entry to the railway museum at Oxenhope whilst there is a nominal fee payable by other visitors. In the shed are many old engines, rolling stock, redundant railway signs, station labels and other machinery. Our favourite item here is the Pullman carriage which is laid out in 1930s style ready for a full scale dinner. It is possible to book dinner on occasions when the Pullman is brought out onto the line and the meal served as in days of yore. The White Rose Pullman Evenings are something special with diners joining the train at 19.10 hrs at Oxenhope, and at 19.30 the train steams away for a three hour trip of nostalgia up and down the line. There is also the Pullman Car 'Mary' restored to grandeur of the 1930s, but this costs more than eating in the 1950s restaurant car. A stop is made to allow diners to enjoy 'Oakworth by Gaslight' and by the time Oxenhope station is reached the platform is also lit by gas thus keeping 'that old feeling' right to the end of this memorable trip.

This railway, however, is not only for the adults or the gourmet — it is a joy to watch the children travelling by the power of steam for the first time! Those of us who remember the old railways hated getting soot in our hair and grit in our eyes. Modern kids find it worth a smile and their delighted chuckles echo in the shops, the waiting rooms and the engine sheds.

The line is open daily during the summer months and at weekends in winter. Enquiries should be directed to the Society

The old booking office has been retained on the Worth Valley line.

Headquarters at Haworth or by telephone on (0535)43629 (talking timetable) or (0535)45214 (general enquiries). The Society produces a quarterly magazine called 'Push and Pull'.

This is by far the best way to travel to Haworth and this was the route followed by Mrs Gaskell, the biographer of Charlotte Brontë. Just as Holmfirth would be unknown to many tourists without *'The Last of the Summer Wine'* Haworth would be nothing without the Brontës and the Parsonage Museum is one of the most frequently visited attractions in the Pennines. This is the last place one would expect controversy and yet during the early 1990s the Brontë Society had such a major internal disagreement that its ferocity reached the national newspapers. It concerned an extension to the museum which everyone agreed was required. The difference concerned what form it should take. Should the extension be attached to the house the Brontës knew so well or would it be better to leave the original alone and construct an underground extension? We hope that the latter scheme prevails because we so enjoy the atmosphere generated by the old building. The shop in

incline down to Appleby and then to Long Marton, Newbiggin, Culgaith, Langwathby, Little Salkeld, Lazonby, Armathwaite, Cotehill, Cumwhinton and Scotby. Beyond this the line joined the Carlisle to Newcastle route at Petterill Bridge on the outskirts of Carlisle. Travelling on the Settle-Carlisle is a joy and enables the architecture and the landscape to be studied. This is stonewall country but also the typical farmhouses and barns can be studied. The outlying barns tend to have doorways with a high circular arch to enable loads of hay to be driven in without getting so wet that storage became a problem. The Dalesfolk certainly thought ahead.

The line was a magnificent feat of engineering, a tribute to the designer's expertise and the endurance of those whose sheer muscle performed the physical work. The 2,629 feet (800 metres) long Blea Moor Tunnel was particularly difficult to build and keeping it free from water seepage is still an expensive business.

Apart from a hard-working period during and between the two wars the Settle-Carlisle has seldom been free from the threat of closure during which time the many railway companies became rationalised into four companies. These were the Southern, Great Western, The London and North Eastern and the London Midland and Scottish which absorbed the Settle-Carlisle. Even in the days when mighty locomotives were being built it still took two engines to negotiate the long drag and this led to the establishment of sidings at Ais Gill where the surplus engines could be detached and travelled back 'light' to Carlisle or Hellifield. At Garsdale there was the only junction along the whole line which linked with Hawes and the route down Wensleydale which has now sadly closed. This route was built by the North Eastern Railway and later absorbed into the London and North Eastern Region network. A good friend of our parents was a signalman on the Settle to Carlisle in the days of steam and he told us that there was a turntable at Garsdale which was protected by a huge pile of heavy sleepers to stop the fierce Pennine winds from catching the engines during the turn round and literally spinning them like a top. He also told us that the same winds were known to keep the signalman stranded in his box and even stop trains from crossing the Ribblehead viaduct. Not only was the Settle-Carlisle an expensive line to build but it was and still is expensive to maintain, with many settlements sited long distances from their station, the prime example being the charming village of Dent. Here was born Adam Sedgewick who became professor of geology at Cambridge, no doubt influenced in his studies to some extent by the cuttings associated with the Settle to Carlisle. Low profit levels, however, made the LMS railway company think of closing the line in the 1930s and once the national network had been nationalised the threat was almost continual especially after the closure of the Hawes branch in 1959. Further problems arose in 1969 when the Waverley route from Carlisle to Edinburgh was closed and that meant re-routing the traffic along the Settle-Carlisle but at the same time many stations were closed and only Appleby and Settle continued to be staffed.

Throughout the 1980s there was a threat to close the line at least once every couple of years; walkers and naturalists objected but travelled to the protest meetings in their cars; villages who were two car families grumbled that they would feel isolated. The fact that the line should be regarded as a working national museum and its associated tourist potential were probably instrumental in saving the line. In 1990 the Settle-Carlisle was at last declared to be safe and we can only hope that some effort is made to restore some of the stations. The route is an ideal place from which to explore Malhamdale also called Upper Airedale and the Three Peaks all of which are best explored on foot. Airedale gave its name to a dog which had its use on the river having been bred around 1865 by crossing a terrier with an otter hound. One of our grandfathers used to breed Airedales, the largest of the terriers and we have fond memories of the faithful Nell his breeding bitch who had the sweetest of temperaments.

After a long stretch of dark millstone grit the Pennines now return to gloriously pale limestone which we last saw around Castleton in Derbyshire. The scenery begins to change around Skipton with Airton and Kirkby Malham both worth a brief halt on the way up the dale to Malham; the road is good and a meandering footpath follows the river. Airton has no pub but it does have a Quaker Meeting House built around 1700 and

Ribblehead Station with Whernside in the background. The station would make a splendid museum and Information Centre and should not be allowed to fall into ruin.

has an associated burial ground whilst even earlier buildings are the post office dated 1666 and the manor house of 1668. Whilst there is nothing unique about any of these buildings, the so-called squatters house situated close to the stocks on the village green is almost unique. In medieval times any homeless person could obtain the right to construct a dwelling on common land providing smoke was issuing from a hearth within 24 hours of the commencement of work. Whilst the Airton house has been developed since its foundation it is a fascinating link with an ancient right.

The parish church of the Dale is, as its name implies, at Kirkby Malham and may have been established in Saxon times but the present building dates to the 15th century. There was an extensive restoration in 1879, during which a three decker pulpit was sadly removed. Many historians visit the church to look at two signatures which were almost certainly written by Oliver Cromwell whilst attending marriages. It is known that in 1655 Cromwell stayed with General Lambert who lived at Calton Hall above Airton. Apparently there used to be a ducking stool near the church although this has now gone but the stocks remain in the churchyard.

Beyond the church is Malham itself snuggled into the limestone scenery although millstone grit asserts itself just occasionally. Malham is an important halt along the Pennine Way. On 24 April 1965 the whole route was officially opened here, and no area deserved the honour more as it has three special places — the Cove, the Scar and the Tarn. Malham Cove is famous for its echo and in high summer it seems almost to overflow with visitors. A surprisingly small stream trickles crystal clear from the foot of the 240 foot (73 metre) high amphitheatre. This area of Malhamdale is more reminiscent of Derbyshire peakland than any other. The formation is due to ancient earth movements along the Craven fault where rocks to the north were pushed upwards against those from the south. Water once flowed over the cliff in what must have been a dramatic waterfall, but the upland porous limestone has swallowed the flow and it emerges below the cove. Close by is the equally famous Gordale Scar which is a gorge caused by the collapse of a cavern and more than 250 feet (76 metres) deep and this is waterfall country with one of the most dramatic being Janet's Foss pouring over a wide but fairly low apron of limestone. Below the fall a footpath leads through a narrow but luxuriant area of woodland rich in ferns, spring flowers and breeding birds including treecreeper, redstart, tawny owl, great spotted woodpecker and an assortment of warblers which arrive during March and April.

Malham Tarn is the highest stretch of inland water in the Pennines being aroud 1,229 feet (374 metres) above sea level. The area is under the protection of the National Trust and there is also a study centre run by the Field Studies Council based upon Malham Tarn House built by Walter Morrison in 1850 and who enjoyed its seclusion for the last 64 years of his life. Walter was no recluse, however, and for 40 years he sat in the Houses of Parliament. His friends often gathered to enjoy the local scenery and to discuss their work and here came John Ruskin, John Stuart Mill, Charles Darwin and Charles Kingsley began writing *The Water Babies* whilst staying with Walter Morrison. He made good use of the local Pennine scenery and a careful study of the book will enable the reader to recognise many areas including Malham Cove. The Pennine Way actually passes through the grounds of Malham Tarn House which have also been laid out as a nature trail. The tarn itself provides excellent bird watching, especially in the winter. It is the water emerging from the tarn which sinks into the limestone to produce a dry valley. The sink holes mark the point where impervious shales come in contact with the limestone. The latter has become dissolved by the water and the shales, which also form the bed of Malham tarn, are much more resistant. The shales were formed during Silurian times which began about 435 million years ago whereas limestone was laid down between 395 and 345 million years ago.

There is a National Park centre with a large car park in the village and which has excellent audio visual presentations concerned with this area of the Pennines and there are books, postcards and leaflets on sale. There is usually some free literature available giving the dates of local events such as sheep dog trials, exhibitions of stone walling and guided walks.

From Malham there is a delightful walk over the moors to Settle whilst the Pennine Way itself is equally attractive and leads over Fountains Fell which is about 1,650 feet (503 metres) above sea level. The path crosses Tennant Gill and then on to Horton-in-Ribblesdale via Penyghent the first of the famous three peaks. The whole area is famous for its splendid limestone pavements with its typical flora such as shining cranesbill and hart's tongue fern.

The name Penyghent derives from the Celtic pen y cant meaning the hill of the border country, pen meaning a hill and cant meaning a rim. Other workers are equally confident that it means 'hill of the winds' and we find it difficult to argue with either definition. This is certainly stormy country and since 1930 periods of heavy rain have exposed screes of millstone grit which also form a cap on top of what is a huge slab of limestone soaring 2,273 feet (694 metres) above Upper Ribblesdale. Snow can lie late in these areas and the mountain is best seen from Horton-in-Ribblesdale especially from the main road in front of the church of St Oswald. The present building is Norman in origin although there was an extensive restoration around 1400 when the tower was built; in the west window the tower is a fragment of stained glass which was brought from Jervaulx

The Pennine Way crosses Penyghent and the village of Horton-in-Ribblesdale is a popular place for hikers to take a rest.

Abbey in Wensleydale which was dissolved by Henry VIII in the late 1530s. It depicts the head of Thomas à Becket whose martyrdom was commemorated by the monks. Anyone wishing to meet climbers, pot holers and Pennine Way walkers should enjoy a snack at the Penyghent cafe or a pint at the Crown. There is some bed and breakfast available and a number of good camping and caravan sites. Botanists also find Penyghent fascinating especially for the carpets of purple saxifrage which grows well on the slopes.

Ingleborough is 2,373 feet (723 metres) and is the second of the three peaks. The third of the trio is the highest and Whernside is 2,419 feet (736 metres) but it has a less dramatic shape and seems to be the least dominant. To the naturalist the Whernside tarns are of great interest, although they are small. Situated at the northern end of the mountain the marshland around the water provides a perfect habitat for a colony of breeding black headed gulls. The three mountains are linked by their own footpath of some 27 miles and there is now an annual fell race over the route the record being 2 hours 29 minutes and 53 seconds — a phenomenal time when you consider the time of a marathon which is only a little shorter. The idea of the three peaks path was the idea of a couple of masters from Giggleswick school way back in July 1887 when they covered the route at night. We have been on each of the three summits in moonlight and on one special night we sat on the flat summit of Ingleborough and looked down at the illuminations of Morecambe and Blackpool reflected in the waters of the Irish Sea. The top of this mountain is so flat that it is said that a game of football could be played on the plateau. Hockey has certainly been played and horse races were also once held up here in the clouds. There is a viewing indicator on the summit placed there by the Ingleton Fell rescue team to celebrate the Coronation of Elizabeth II in 1953.

Just as at Castleton in the Peak District the Pennine explorer can enjoy the underground features of a limestone district with Ingleton Cave and White Scar caverns open to the public. Ingleton cave despite its name is best reached from the attractive little village of Clapham whilst the White Scar system is situated between Ingleton and Ribblehead. Ingleton is also waterfall country with a splendid walk running from the village around Thornton force. An entry fee is required for all these three attractions and all provide a shop and a cafe during the season.

From Ingleton the Romans built a road to connect with their fort at Bainbridge some 19 miles to the north and its route can be traced leaving Ingleton between Kingsdale Beck and the River Greta, passing over Cam Fell and Dodd Hill and down to Gayle near Hawes. Dodd Fell at 1,877 feet (572 metres) lies astride an old green track running in a north-easterly direction and walkers find this conveniently close to Hawes which caters well for walkers and campers and usually more demanding tourists. Close to Hawes is the village of Hardraw with its famous waterfall and which lies directly on the Pennine Way. Lovers of the old Dales know that the walk from Hawes towards Middleton-in-Teesdale leads out of the West Riding through the East Riding and into County Durham. We all regret the passing of the Ridings. Some of the best scenery is to be found in Swaledale, with Thwaite and Keld being of particular interest.

Thwaite will be forever known as the home base for the Kearton brothers whose working life extended over the turn of the 20th century; Richard was best known as a naturalist but

Ingleborough's flat summit is apparently smooth enough to be used as a sports field.

the younger brother Cherry pioneered wildlife photography both still and on movie film. The hills around provided them with inspiration. The village has made full use of the tourist potential of the Keartons and tea shops abound whilst up the dale at Keld there is a youth hostel. Its welcoming doors and the smell of good food cooking must be irresistable to walkers, especially those on the way from Thwaite, who have just climbed Kisdon Hill, 1,636 feet (499 metres) above sea level and crossing the old corpse way down into Muker. Corpse ways were a feature of the remote areas of the Pennines which had a widespread, often isolated populations, and with churches few and far between. Bodies had to be taken for burial along well recognised pathways.

Keld was once an important lead mining centre and an old smelting mill still stands close to the Pennine Way. The tiny village with its attractive cluster of grey cottage also has its beauty and is within range of several attractive waterfalls including Wain Wath Force and a series of rippling cascades over Kisdon Gorge. After heavy rain or snow melt which are not uncommon in this area of upper Swaledale, Kisdon Force can be really dramatic. The Swale rises above Keld and tumbles quickly down between banks of limestone.

From Keld the Pennine Way runs to Stainmore a distance of ten miles and passing Tan Hill which at 1,732 feet (528 metres) is the highest licenced premises in England; whether it is the most remote is open to debate as Pennine walkers may feel that the Cat and Fiddle around the headwaters of the Goyt and the Snake Inn may both lay claim to this dubious honour. Six hundred years ago they were mining coal up here and which supplied fuel for Richmond Castle and also the homes of Lady Anne Clifford at Skipton, Barden, Pendragon and Appleby which are described in the next chapter. In the 17th century another indefatigable lady named Celia Fiennes described in her diary how the coal was won 'They also have engines that draw up their coale in sort of baskets in a well, for their mines are dug down through a sort of well and sometimes its pretty low before they come to the coales.' The pits are now closed but at one time the Inn had its own shaft and round about were the 'shops' or 'bothies' in which the colliers lived. The Inn itself, restored and extended in 1990, used to be called King's Pit House, dates to the 18th century and its outbuildings were once ale houses in their own right, a sure sign of the prolific thirst of the colliers.

There are splendid views from an outcrop at the back of the Inn with Shunner Fell above Hawes quite prominent and the smudge of industry which still sometimes covers Middlesborough on the Tees estuary can also be seen on a good day even though it is around 50 miles away. From the Inn the Pennine Way crosses Sleightholme Moor which is only about 1,200 feet (366 metres) but it is quite exposed and is something of a slog. We much prefer to cover this area of the Pennines by car but Stainmore, which means stony land, can certainly not be missed. Stainmore is a vital Pennine crossing and the first major route to be crossed since Gargrave. The A66 linking Penrith with Scotch Corner is often as busy as the M62 lower down the Pennines but without the benefit of bridges across it and is thus something of a pedestrian's nightmare. One fascinating feature of Stainmore is the so-called God's Bridge which is a natural limestone span over the river Greta which here is subterranean, except after periods of heavy rain.

From Stainmore we found ourselves with something of a problem — the Pennine Way is narrow whilst the Pennines themselves are obviously much wider; obviously we had to backtrack a little to cover firstly the haunts of Lady Anne Clifford then to explore Teesdale via what has been known as the Bowes loop and also Upper Weardale before returning to the main line of the Pennine Way from Dufton over Cross Fell to Alston.

CHAPTER 8

Anne Clifford — a great Pennine Lady

If the women's movement ever needs a patron saint they need look no further than Lady Anne Clifford, born in the time of the first Elizabeth when men ruled the whole universe. Perhaps Elizabeth herself inspired an early awakening of womens lib. For those on the lookout for a guide through the Pennine Dales of Yorkshire, then this indefatigable landowner and traveller is perfect. Born at Skipton castle on 30 January 1590 Anne was the third but only surviving child of George Clifford the Third Earl of Cumberland, and his wife Margaret Russel. Anne, who was only 4 feet 10 inches in height spent most of her early years in London where she was well educated — for a woman at least — but she never lost her love of the Pennine countryside. When she was 15 her father died and she was devastated when his lands passed not to her but to her uncle and thereafter to his son. Anne, encouraged by her mother, challenged the will but all efforts failed and she only inherited when she was 60 following the death of her cousin who was childless. Meanwhile she had become a rich woman in her own right and twice widowed, although neither of her husbands was enlightened enough to overtly support her personal claims. Her first marriage was to the frivolous Earl of Dorset by whom she had five children, although only two daughters survived. Later she married Philip the Earl of Pembroke and when he died in 1650 Anne set off north to claim her inheritance and set about restoring the Clifford estates with phenomenal energy. This was at the time of Cromwell's Republic and orders were issued forbidding the strengthening of fortified buildings. Not only did this tough lady ignore these instructions, but she advertised her part in their reconstruction by inserting huge inscribed blocks many of which have survived to the present day. When she died in 1676 at the age of 86 the Clifford estates were in a fine state of repair. Even during her 80s Lady Anne was travelling miles over rough trans-Pennine roads to oversee works on her estates.

101

Lady Anne Clifford.

It is possible to trace her journeys and we began our pilgrimage in her footsteps at Skipton castle the place of her birth.

Skipton castle is open every day of the year except Christmas day. Around the time that Lady Anne was born Skipton castle was being renovated, but by the time she returned it had been knocked about more than a bit by the opposing armies of the Civil War. It was soon made habitable and the motto '*Desormais*' carved in stone over the entrance which it still dominates. Beneath the castle some signs of the moat can be seen, but the stretch of water visible is actually the Springs branch of the Leeds to Liverpool canal which was described in chapter four. Although the castle had its own chapel Lady Anne was at great pains to restore the Parish church situated at the foot of the castle. Many family monuments of the Clifford family are here, some removed from nearby Bolton Priory at the Dissolution of the monasteries on the orders of Henry VIII in the late 1530s. The main restoration of the church was completed by 1655 and also about this time she completed the building of Beamsley

Hospital a fine set of alms houses which had been begun by her mother, also a most formidable lady. Lady Margaret Russel (1560–1616) had married George Clifford in 1577 a union blessed by the presence of Queen Elizabeth. Margaret was a very clever woman interested in alchemy and was apparently also a very skilled herbalist. She fought hard to ensure her daughter's inheritance and there was apparently a loving bond between them — two women brave enough to challenge the world of men. The alms houses are a fitting memorial to the pair, the round chapel being unique. This is surrounded by a number of dwellings which are now owned by the Landmark Trust who let them out as holiday homes. It is a pity that they are not still used by the needy as are a set of houses built by Lady Anne at Appleby, but at least they are well maintained and safe for ever.

From Skipton Lady Anne's route into the Pennines took her past Bolton Priory to Barden Tower, one of her favourite houses which had been constructed as a medieval hunting lodge with an attached chapel and priests' house. There is plenty of parking and a rather pleasant restaurant close to the tower. Above what was the entrance Lady Anne recorded the fact that she restored the building in 1657, having a particular affection for the place because her mother had stayed at Barden at the time she was pregnant with Anne.

Below the tower is Barden Bridge where there is also ample parking space. From here there are magnificent walks along both banks of the Wharfe. The sun sparkled on the water as we watched common sandpiper, dipper and grey wagtail all busy claiming food and territory as their breeding season gathered momentum. Flowers were everywhere including primrose, stichwort, violet, speedwell, bluebell and the onion smelling ramsons also known as wild garlic. We have also walked the Wharfe in driving rain when we watched goosanders fishing by diving into the torrent of brown flood water; during the cold winter weather with ice blocks bobbing like corks down the river we once watched a water vole cross from one bank to the other. We thought about Lady Anne as she journeyed up through Buckden, Aysgarth, Bainbridge and on into Hawes, then but a small settlement but now one of the most important stops along the Pennine Way. All this area was described in our

Barden Tower, one of Lady Anne's castles which she lovingly restored.

companion volume *Discovering the Yorkshire Dales*. The searcher after the Pennine Panorama should visit the Information Centre and the Folk Museum situated in the buildings of the station closed during the Beeching cuts of the 1960s. What a pity that those in charge at the time did not see the tourist potential of having a steam railway running up Wensleydale and linking with the Settle-Carlisle line at Garsdale. The Folk Museum, entry to which requires a small fee, houses the collection gathered by Marie Hartley and Joan Ingilby who have written so many learned and in-depth studies of each of the Dales. Lady Anne would have approved of their energies. Hawes is the centre for the manufacture of Wensleydale cheese and walkers can often be seen buying supplies to keep them going during their trek along the Pennine Way. Some keep their heads down and keep walking although others add a few miles to their journey by visiting one of the most famous waterfalls in the country at Hardraw. One of the tributaries of the Ure is Fossdale Beck which rises on Great Shunner Fell and descends steeply to Hardraw about 2 miles to the north of Hawes. It then tumbles over a 100-foot limestone cliff which can be reached by paying a small fee at the bar of the Green Dragon Inn and then out through the back door into a natural amphitheatre. Blondin the tightrope walker famous in Victorian England crossed the gap whilst cooking an omelette! Those of a more sober disposition prefer to follow the footpath which leads behind the waterfall. Lady Anne kept notes of her movements and knew Hawes and beyond this is the source of the Ure and another of its tributaries the Cotter which also has an impressive waterfall. She wrote 'I went over Cotter in my coach (where I think never coach went before) and over Hellgill Bridge into Westmoreland.' Even in the days of good roads and powerful cars this area of Pennines is impressive and dramatic, followed for part of the way by the Settle to Carlisle railway.

Just beyond the Moorcock Inn on the B6259 is another reminder of Lady Anne's travels. Outhgill Chapel at Mallerstang is a joy and Lady Anne loved it so much that she restored it and placed her usual plaque over the door of the building which is dedicated to St Mary. As usual after recording the fact that she paid for the restoration the inscription quotes from Isaiha, Chapter 58, verse 12 which says that 'they shall be of thee shall build the old waste places.' The present chapel is organised from Kirkby Stephen. Few buildings can be so delightfully situated overlooked by fells in an area which in spring rings with bird song. In winter an icy wind can freeze you to the marrow as it blasts off the moors. Pennine winds are notorious and locals call them lazy because they go through you rather than round you!

Just beyond the chapel is yet another castle restored by Lady Anne but alas only a mere shell remains today. Pendragon was restored in 1663 and the family spent Christmas there, the first time that the place had been occupied for more than a century. Pendragon is one of many places in Britain said to have associations with King Arthur. This may or may not be true but what the place does have without question is atmosphere. This was very obvious as we walked around the ruin by following the clearly defined line of the old moat. Rushes still grow in the damper areas and a couple of swallows were busy collecting

Pendragon Castle, although now ruined, was restored by Lady Anne Clifford.

Lady Anne Clifford's plaque on one of her favourite chapels at Mallerstang.

mud with which they were constructing their nest among the crumbling masonry. On one beautiful June morning we watched a fox cub scouting around on what was probably one of its earliest solo excursions. The castle is also surrounded by a number of old ash trees and on the walls grow numerous plants including aubretia and several species of fern including wall rue, rusty-back, polypody and spleenwort. The castle is always open and entry is free.

Lady Anne had a number of other castles in the old county of Westmorland but now in Cumbria which was established in 1974 and described in a companion volume in this series. Those in search of the Pennines, however, should pass through Kirkby Stephen and onto Brough. Kirkby Stephen is a true Pennine town — it even has a Pennine Hotel, and has long been known as a half way stop between the east and west coasts. Coaches will stop here as did the stage coaches in the days of the Turnpikes. The town has the confidence which has developed from being a market for the locals and a welcome stop for the tourists. One establishment which has been a part of the town's business since around 1650 is the Fountain cafe which is now a listed building.

The red sandstone church is of ancient origin, dedicated obviously to St Stephen and built in the 12th century probably on a Saxon base. It was much restored in Victorian times but the Musgrave chapel is a real reminder of medieval times. Here is a recumbent figure of a 15th-century knight and there is a more modern wonder in the form of an engraving by John Hutton, who is particularly well known for his west screen in the new Coventry Cathedral.

On the outskirts of the town is Wharton Hall, now a farmhouse but built in the late 14th or early 15th century. The original design had two cross wings, but in 1540 Thomas Lord Wharton added a new hall, but was also active in the town; in 1566 he founded Kirkby Stephen grammar school.

There are plenty of riverside walks alongside the Eden and many locals choose Mallerstang common as their picnic site; this is situated between Kirkby Stephen and Pendragon castle.

To the north of the town is the historic settlement of Brough which also has connections with Lady Anne Clifford. St Michael's church which was first built in the 11th century, using stones from the old Roman fort. Opposite the church are some old weavers' cottages which once provided the town with its prosperity. There is also a building which was once a Dame's school and a farm which was once an inn used by the packhorse drivers. Set on a nearby hill overlooking a loop of the River Eden is Brough castle built by the Normans but using stones from the Roman fort. The keep is still referred to as the Roman tower. In 1521 the castle was gutted by fire but Lady Anne restored it and the round tower is still known as 'Clifford's Tower'. Lady Anne's own room was situated at the top of the tower and her view over the Eden must have been magnificent.

Brough is actually two villages in one and Market Brough is a picturesque blend of old cobbled courtyards, stables flanking the street, old coaching inns and cottages clustered around a ford which was replaced by a bridge in 1369. This was one of the main routes into the Pennines with one track leading into Middleton-in-Teesdale, an area surprisingly dominated by another traveller — Charles Dickens!

CHAPTER 9

Around Teesdale

This chapter had its origins many years ago as we were travelling between London Euston and Preston on an inter-city train. Pushed down the side of a seat we found a battered copy of Charles Dicken's novel Nicholas Nickleby. It had an introduction providing background information and we discovered that Dickens, along with his illustrator Hablot K. Browne, travelled up to Yorkshire and the result was Dotheboys Hall, Smike and Wackford Squeers. The inspiration he found at Bowes in Teesdale near Barnard Castle where he also stayed.

On a day of glorious sunshine we journeyed through the Yorkshire Dales and into Durham and on finding Bowes we were surprised at how small it was, but what character we found. Overlooked by a castle and the church of St Giles we found lots of lovely cottages and nearby another set which Dickens used as the model for his notorious school. It is still possible to see the old pump and stone trough at which the boys washed out in the freezing cold. There was actually a school here run by one William Shaw and Dickens converted the initials W. S. to Wackford Squeers. In Browne's illustrations there seems to be a resemblance between Squeers and Shaw. The Unicorn Inn was also faithfully described in Nicholas Nickelby as the place where the coach carrying the schoolboys stopped. The novel, published in 1838, was an important social comment and many of the notorious schools in the remote parts of the Pennines miles away from establishments with a conscience and without any pretentions of scholarship were forced to close. William Shaw is buried in Bowes churchyard and there is also the grave of an unfortunate pupil which gave Dickens the idea for the pathetic character of Smike. Actually one poor boy did escape from Shaw's evil academy and reached Lynesack some 12 miles away across the Tees valley before he died. The child must have passed through Cotherstone near which there was another infamous 'Yorkshire School' at Woodencroft. This was attended by Richard Cobden who

Bowes castle showing its moat and with the church in the background.

worked so hard to establish free trade during the mid 19th century. It is reported that his memories of his early education was 'a desolate time of which he could never afterwards endure to speak.'

The origins of Bowes takes us back to Roman times and both the church and the castle are on the site of a fort called Lavatris. Inside St Giles there is the bowl of a Saxon font supported on a small Roman pillar on which the Latin inscriptions are clearly legible. Another reminder of Roman Britain is found in the north trancept and which is very difficult to miss. It is a huge stone slab which was found in the castle grounds in 1929 and has been dated to the 3rd century AD. The fort had the distinction of being the last Roman settlement to be abandoned in these northern parts. A more modern point of interest in the church is a clock placed in position by public subscription in 1897 to commemorate Queen Victoria's Diamond Jubilee. The workings are enclosed in a wooden case with a glass front so that the intricate workings can be seen and the huge instrument ticks so loudly that it echoes throughout the church. It was made by W. Potts and Son of Leeds and it was fascinating to discover that they have regularly serviced the clock ever since and we were able to read the signatures of those who had attended to it the last being dated 13 December 1990.

Close to the church are the ruins of the castle which are used by a colony of breeding jackdaws and on a glorious June day of blue sky and buzzing bumble bees we wondered what Dickens thought of the ancient pile on the days of his January visit. Now preserved by English Heritage and freely open daily the castle was built around 1175. It played a significant part in defending England against invading Scots and even in its present ruinous state the deep but dry moat and towering walls look formidable. It did, however, fail to resist the skillful and fearless attacks of Robert the Bruce around 1322. It never recovered from its capture and sacking and in the 17th century it was used as an unofficial quarry but the basic layout of its Norman foundation can still be seen. A solitary horsechestnut stands in the grounds and in this we watched a graceful little treecreeper work its way in a spiral up the trunk in search of insects under the bark and looking from a distance just like a clockwork mouse.

Some time ago we paused near the church and asked a local the way to Bowes museum only to be told that it had nothing to do with the village but was part of Barnard Castle a much larger market town overlooking a broad twist in the River Tees.

Our best memory among many visits to Barnard Castle is of a breakfast eaten in the picnic site below the castle. The dew was still glistening in the grass and a couple of horses soaked up the morning sunshine and cropped away contentedly at the lush greenery. From the mighty castle the English Heritage flag fluttered gently in the breeze, and people were already winding their way up the steep winding path from the narrow 14th-century bridge over the river to the castle and the town sited on the hill towering above it.

If Bowes is a surprisingly quiet backwater then Barnard Castle is also a surprise, but for the opposite reason. The gentle climb to the castle entrance can often be negotiated in silence but beyond this is like ringing up the curtain of a theatre with a cast of hundreds if not thousands. The castle is early Norman and founded by Guy de Balliol but substantially rebuilt by his nephew Bernard around 1150. Bernard's was a

St Giles Church, Bowes.

massive and influential castle on the edge of the Pennines.
It occupied 6½ acres and its most impressive remnant is the
Round Tower which dates to the 14th century. From this there
are delightful views down over the Tees which inspired Sir
Walter Scott when he was writing *Rokeby*, published in 1813; it
is a poem of six cantos set around Greta Bridge after the battle
of Marston Moor which was fought in 1644. Barnard Castle also
inspired the painter J. M. W. Turner who made four working
tours around the Pennines including Teesdale, Swaledale and
Wensleydale. The first was in 1797 when he was 22, the second
and third in 1816 and 1817, when he worked on watercolours
for histories of Yorkshire and Durham. The fourth took place
in 1831 when Turner's commission was to illustrate sites used in
the works of Sir Walter Scott and hence his visit to the Barnard
Castle area. The castle is open on most days of the year and
a fee is payable at the kiosk which also sells guide books both
to the castle and the district. Occasionally medieval pageants
and mock battles take place and if only stones could speak we
wonder what delight they would express at these returns to the
glory days.

In the town itself are several fine old inns including the Kings Head, where Dickens probably stayed whilst researching Nicholas Nickleby, and also a journal story called 'Master Humphrey's Clock'. There is a plaque near the market cross and buttermarket topped by a fire bell where one of the two shops owned by Humphrey Grey the clockmaker once stood. The covered market cross itself is substantial and once served as both the town hall and the lock-up. Beyond this is the church of St Mary's which to us is rather disappointing although described as Norman and Transitional. There is a chapel dedicated to St Margaret of Scotland no doubt dating to the days of border squabbles. Although we could not find a church guide we did find reference to two English Kings on the 15th-century chancel arch leading into the raised chapel. One pillar depicts the head of Edward IV (1461–1483) and the ill-fated Richard III (1483–1485) is depicted on another.

Quite close to, and signed from the market cross is Bowes museum which was built in the style of a French Chateau and is full of European paintings and furniture. It is a huge building some 300 feet long and 130 feet wide which, although it was built in 1869 it looks distinctly 17th century. John Bowes and his French wife Josaphine built the house to display their invaluable collections, and it is fitting that such an effort to preserve all that is good in the past, should now commemorate their name. There is free parking but an entrance fee to the museum itself, which is open all the year except the week before Christmas and on New Year's Day.

From the market cross another street called the Bank descends to the river passing Blagraves House which is now a restaurant. It is a four-storeyed Tudor house in which it is said, probably with some truth, in 1648 Cromwell was entertained, being given mulled wine and shortcake. On Thorngate there are some 18th-century houses which have played their part in the history of the town with their long top floor windows indicating the days when first simple weaving and then carpet manufacture were the staple industries.

There are lovely walks along the river bank both to Thorngate and also to the ruins of Egglestone abbey which so impressed Turner as he painted its ruins. It still gives the impression of beauty combined with strength and a lovely atmosphere

The font in St Giles church, at Bowes, is a real hybrid with a Norman Bowl on a stem which was once a Roman altar.

of peace generated by centuries of prayer. Here the Tees is crossed by a single-arch stone bridge with a battlemented parapet producing a medieval look to it even though it was constructed in 1773. There is, however, an older packhorse bridge over the Thornsgill beck which the monks diverted, culverted and managed to provide a water supply for their abbey. The brethren belonged to the Premonstratensian order, their mother house being close to Richmond in Swaledale. The founder was Robert de Malton in 1196. Later the order was absorbed by the Cistercians, but unlike other Cistercian abbeys Egglestone never became important and was dissolved by Henry VIII in 1540. In 1548 it was purchased by Robert Strelley who built a house on the east side of the ruins. All that remains of the Abbey are parts of the cruciform church, but the real joy is the approach along the Tees through lovely woodlands full of delightful flowers and a variety of birds, including woodcock, tawny owl, and great spotted woodpecker, all being resident, whilst in summer they are joined by chiff-chaff, blackcap, wood warbler, and spotted flycatcher.

If following the Dickens' trail brings the history of the area into sharp focus then the upper reaches of Teesdale is one of the finest natural areas left in Europe. Its wildlife and especially its botany has survived despite threats which have now slackened although the flood of potentially heavy footed tourists needs careful control. Teesdale's list of rare plants is endless and out of a species list of around 150 the most notable are the bog sandwort, shrubby cinquefoil and the delightful deep blue spring gentian which seems to be everyone's favourite. We also love the delicate pink blooms of bird's eye primrose, a much more common species and the golden blooms of marsh marigold which cover many of the low lying meadows during early spring. It is also called the kingcup and is a very primitive plant having no petals, the bright colour being due to the lovely shiny sepals which protect the reproductive organs prior to the bud bursting. It is thought that the marsh marigold was one of the first plants to colonise Britain following the retreat of the ice and in Teesdale's harsh climate it is growing in its primitive environment. Those who come for scenery rather than flowers are not disappointed with High Force and Cauldron Snout being exciting waterfalls overlooked by high fells including Cronkley and Widdybanks.

This is real walkers' country and one of the toughest stretches of the Pennine Way punches its way through Upper Teesdale. Many a weary traveller heaves a sigh of relief when the Langden Beck Youth Hostel comes into view. They have little time to seek out the signs of old stone circles, Iron Age huts, the hill forts of the Brigantes a tribe of Ancient Britons or for reminders of the Roman occupations.

Barnard Castle is situated above the river Tees and among delightful countryside.

Close by is Cross Fell, which at 2,930 feet (893 metres) is the highest point of the Pennine range and this along with South Gare mark the two extremes of the River Tees, surely one of the hardest working rivers of the world. On its lower banks have developed huge chemical complexes feeding greedily on the salt-based chemicals deposited during the evaporation caused by a period of tropical weather, of the Shallow Zechstein sea some 250 million years ago. Industry is still a feature of the lower reaches of the Tees, but the Upper Dale has a wild unpolluted feel about it. A closer look, however, reveals the scars of industry which was made possible about 100 million years ago when earth movements lifted rocks above the limestone and these were found to contain lead, zinc, flourspar and barytes and formed as part of the hard black Whin Sill. Upper Teesdale shares these minerals with other areas of the Pennines, but it has one unique feature of its own. A molten sheet of rock, the Great Whin Sill, intruded deep into the limestone and coal measures and it can be seen as a hard edge to waterfalls and has been quarried all along the dale. It is found as black basalt flutes similar to that found on the Giant's causeway in Ireland or the Island of Staffa which Mendelsohn made famous in Fingal's Cave, part of his Hebridean Overture. This hot sheet of Whin Sill had the effect of literally baking some of the rocks to form sugar limestone which is granular and drained very quickly. Its structure prevents the roots of trees from establishing themselves and the areas remained open thus allowing the tough arctic plants so typical of Upper Teesdale to survive.

Once the plant life had gained a root-hold animals were able to move into the area and the combination of the two enabled human tribes to colonise what is now Upper Teesdale. Settlers arrived in the middle Stone Age wending their way through damp woodland valleys and up onto the catchment area for the river which teemed with fish. Then came a change in climate with cool wet conditions replacing warmer drier weather. Prior to this change even some elms had grown on Cross Fell, but these soon died and over a period of time heavy rainfall fell on the tree-less moorland and leached out all the minerals needed for good plant growth and large areas of acid peat bog developed. By around 2000 BC Upper Teesdale looked much

The centre of Barnard Castle has changed very little since Charles Dickens stayed in and wrote about the town.

as it does today with areas of plant refuges which have always been rare enough to be vulnerable. There were also lowland areas where the soil was more fertile and the environment more protected from the elements. Even where the woodland was felled it soon regenerated and there are a good number of these still standing especially in the areas around Holwick and High Force; Juniper grows well here and its berries were used to flavour gin whilst its timber was then used to produce the finest gunpowder.

Conservation is not a modern invention but has been part of the life of Upper Teesdale since 1131 when an Act was passed forbidding grazing in unenclosed areas of woodland between November 11 and April 1 when all animals had to be kept in what was defined as in-by land are fed on hay. In 1218 much land was owned by the Cistercian monks of Rievaulx Abbey and they realised the activities of lead and silver mining were potentially in conflict with farming and wildlife. The pursuit of profit, however, is usually irresistable and so Teesdale became an important focus of the mining industry based in and around Middleton-in-Teesdale. Middleton is often referred to as the capital of Upper Teesdale but as it is only ten miles from Barnard Castle some historians point out that it is only a large village whilst others insist that it is a market town. It is hard to argue with the latter as there was once a Market Place, a Horsemarket, a Town Hall and a Shambles. Let us settle for an old lead mining centre and an ideal base for exploring some of the finest Pennine scenery and lying almost on the Pennine Way itself. With the decline of lead mining Middleton's fortunes rested very heavily upon farming but in recent years tourism has become an important source of income to the valley. Obviously there are occasions when the two are in direct conflict but there is now more mutual understanding between farming, tourism and conservation. This was certainly not the case when Cow Green Reservoir was constructed in the 1970s. The battle to prevent the flooding of part of the Dale to slake the thirst of the expanding industries of Teesmouth was lost. An important geological feature, the famous Weel of the Tees vanished beneath the waters as did a number of important plant communities. Despite the damage it caused there can be no doubt that Cow Green itself is now an area of beauty being a two mile expanse of open water much frequented by water birds and from it there are splendid views of the Pennine hills especially from the Weelhead Sike car park from which the most prominent land mark is Cross Fell.

Middleton-in-Teesdale is an ideal place to explore all these areas, but the settlement itself deserves much more than a passing glance. The name Middleton means that here was a 'middle settlement' which is probably its original Anglo-Saxon name, the 'in-Teesdale' extension having to be added as other Middletons evolved in the high Pennines and elsewhere. There is documentary evidence of its existence along with Raby and Staindrop which are described in the next chapter, during the reign of Canute (Cnut) around AD 1030 at which time he also ruled Denmark.

Historians argue about which area of Middleton is the most ancient but nobody argues about its haunting beauty as its buildings cluster around a hillside overlooking a graceful bridge over the River Tees. Despite the lead mining industry it remained attractive although some evidence of the old workings remains. It was the hard working Quakers who developed

High Force is one of the most dramatic waterfalls in Britain.

the London Lead Company around the mid 18th century and influence was profound until the early 20th century. Unlike the lead-hungry owners in other areas the faith of the Quakers ensured a more benevolent attitude to their workers. They provided compact cottages for the miners not only in Middleton itself but close to the workings throughout the Dale. The maximum use was made of space by siting the cottages on terraces. Although the present church of St Mary was built in 1876 there are reminders of earlier religious structures within it and around it. There is a detached bell tower which is 16th century and one of its three bells is dated 1558. There are some stone carvings and medieval stone grave covers plus a rather attractive piscina in which the sacramental vessels were washed. Outside is a cross which once dominated village activities and near which once stood the stocks.

Near the church is what may be described as one of the first pre-fabs in the world. It is called the Grant Lodge and it was transported from Norway to be exhibited in the Crystal Palace Great Exhibition of 1851. It was moved to Middleton after the exhibition.

Above all, however, this is walking country and nearby are some of the most spectacular waterfalls in Britain. A good starting point is at Bowlees picnic site which has excellent parking near a Visitors' Centre which contains displays of mining and other industries which were typical of both Teesdale and Weardale obviously including lead mining but also the extraction of flourspar for steel-making. The wildlife displays are also impressive and there is a nature trail leading from the centre and which is described in a leaflet which is on sale. The gentle stroll leads through woodlands alongside Bowlees Beck and passing an area where visitors are allowed to try their hand at dry stone walling. Around an old limestone quarry ash trees grow in profusion, whilst in the workings themselves bird's foot trefoil, heath orchid and butterwort all grow and the common blue butterfly occurs along with green veined white and small tortoiseshell. Dipper and grey wagtail are both common along the swift moving stream, which picks up pace following a 20 foot drop at Summerhill Force beneath Gibson's cave which is a deeply undercut overhang. Geologists love this area as it is possible to note the changes of rock through shales, sandstone and limestone all carved out by melt-water at the conclusion of the Ice Ages. Three other waterfalls can be reached from Bowlees; Low Force with the Wynch Bridge crossing the Tees, the dramatic High Force probably the most popular with visitors and Cauldron Snout.

We have never seen High Force other than impressive but after heavy rain it is spectacular, a 70 foot drop over the black cliff of the Great Whin Sill. At flood times there is a second drop close to the main force and in winter there are special days when the water freezes into a cascade of icicles. A wooded path leads down from an extensive car park near the High Force hotel and for which a fee must be paid. The money, however, is well spent on the paths and viewing platforms.

Cauldron Snout is more difficult to reach being situated off the B6277 road at Langden Beck. This waterfall is a 200 foot staircase rather than a sheer drop, and the water feeding it once emerged from the twisting pool known as the weel and as we have seen earlier, now drowned beneath Cow Green reservoir. The falls are said to be haunted by 'The Singing Lady' a young girl who drowned herself in the waters after being spurned by a faithless lead miner.

Anyone wishing to study the history of lead mining in these Northern Pennines must visit Upper Weardale in general and the Killhope Wheel in particular.

Dufton lies on the Pennine Way but is usually quiet enough to provide those wishing to sample a day's hike with an ideal base. Just outside the village and well signed is a narrow track which slowly narrows to form a spiralling footpath. It passes between Knock Fell and Dufton Pike and this is at its best in June when the larks sing and the cuckoo's call can be heard above the chuckle of Great Rundale Beck, on which dipper and common sandpiper both breed, whilst oyster catchers have also raised young in the last few years. In the old days this was lead mining country and the Pennine Way now follows the old mine road to Swindale Beck and from its name we may guess that before the trees were felled wild pigs probably grazed in the sparse woodlands. If this beck is followed, first the well named Green Fell and then the summit of Knock Fell 2,604 feet (794 metres), yet another substantial mountain, is reached. For the day tripper this will probably be sufficient as to continue on to Alston would be far too strenuous because those with cars would obviously have to retrace their steps. We have on occasions joined forces with friends and operated a shuttle service by leaving one car at Alston and the other at Dufton. There is much on Knock Fell, however, to pursuade the naturalist to linger as the Moorhouse National Nature Reserve set up in 1952 by the Nature Conservancy Council takes in 10,000 acres (4,047 hectares) of Pennine moorland. The botanical interest of Knock Fell, Milburn Forest and Dufton Fell is considerable and there are a number of species of club moss and spring sandwort proving that it is one of the few plants which actually love lead in the soil by growing on the old spoil heaps.

A much more controversial development has taken place on Great Dun Fell during the 1980s as a long range radar tracking station was rebuilt to replace an obsolete system dating back to the 1940s. It is far from easy building anything in these parts let alone tall structures such as these which will have to withstand winds of up to 120 knots (75 mph) and temperature falling to below −22°C. One feature of the complex looks just like a huge golf ball on top of the fell which is a great help in enabling the traveller to recognise Great Dun Fell.

Some eight miles of tough walking from Dufton comes Little Dun Fell and the rather unimpressive source of the Tees in a mass of bog and sphagnum moss and then to the top of Cross

The village of Dufton with a wisp of smoke rising from the chimney of the Stag Inn.

Fell the highest point in the Pennine range. It takes its name, according to most authorities, because St Augustine erected a cross on the summit to scare away the evil spirits said to haunt it. Visit Cross Fell on a bad day and one can be forgiven for thinking that Augustine failed, for it is here that the famous Helm Wind is generated and it can sound like the Hounds of Hell. The Helm has fascinated all and frightened many of visitors to this area of Northern Cumbria and we can vouch for its force and remember three occasions in July, January and March when it froze us to the bone and on the second occasion actually confined us to our car which rocked alarmingly and we could not open the door. Perhaps this was a good thing. The dangerous winds usually blow from an easterly or north easterly direction. It is caused by heavy cold air falling down the slopes of Cross Fell into the valley of the River Eden. The descent warms the air and produces whirlpools which, as they spiral upwards and condense, create what is known as the Helm Bar. The ferocity is very much a local phenomenon and never penetrates as far as the River Eden itself — perhaps it is because it is so restricted which has caused the Helm to become such an infamous wind.

The route over Cross Fell is strenuous even in the context of the Pennine Way and passes close to Fallow Hill although the name is something of a misnomer since at 2,583 feet (787 metres) is very much a mountain. Walkers should beware of

disused mine shafts and unstable scree left over from the old
lead workings. After crossing near the line of another Corpse
road, this time running from Carrigill on the South Tyne valley
which did not have a church until the 19th century, with
Kirkland in the Eden valley, being the mother establishment.

The route from Carrigill down to Alston is worth taking
slowly and there is a choice for the walker or the picnicker
who arrives by car. If you look upwards you are often rewarded
by the sighting of curlew, oyster catcher and lapwing. On a
glorious day of warm sunshine we first watched a lapwing
with three tiny young running around its feet and all looking
quite alarmed. At first we thought it was our presence which
had disturbed them, but then we saw a hen harrier hunting
low over the moor with her graceful wing beats carrying her
smoothly over the heathery slopes. This was our first sighting
of a hen harrier in this part of the Pennines although we have
seen them fairly frequently on Pendle and especially on the
Bowland fells. We never forget to look down, however, as the
light often reflects from small crystals of Blue John, the first
time this variety of fluorspar has occurred since Castleton. The
whole of this area is a miner's paradise and ever since Roman
times, and probably long before, zinc, barytes, fluorspar and
especially the richest of the lead ores called galena have been
mined.

For those who wish to discover this remote area by car there
is a perfect route between Dufton and Alston taking in a
string of attractive villages including Knock, Milburn, Blencarn,
Kirkland which was at the end of the corpse road described
above, Skirwith, Ousby and then joining the main road to
Alston at Melmerby. There is then a dramatic journey via the
winding pass of Hartside, at the summit of which is a convenient
hostelry. There is something remarkable about each of these
villages and they are all beautiful so who needs more? Village
greens are a particular feature, and Milburn's is dominated by
a maypole set on the base of an old preaching cross. Scholars
have pointed out that these north country villages are laid out
in a square with their solid cottages facing inwards to provide
protection against marauders from north of the border — cattle
and sheep rustling was not apparently the invention of the Wild
West and neither was the four square construction of a fort.

Even today getting into and out of Milburn involves squeezing through the narrow gaps which could easily be sealed during the Middle Ages.

Few towns are approached through such dramatic scenery as Alston in Cumbria. It seems that the ideal place for the county boundary would be at the top of Hartside pass and indeed Alston seems to us to be more of a Northumbrian than a Cumbrian settlement. The descent from Hartside summit reveals the head stream of the South Tyne river flowing like a ribbon of milk through the dark peat and from the slopes of Cross Fell. Alston at almost 1,000 feet (305 metres) claims to be the highest market town in England, but this is also the boast of Buxton in Derbyshire. Considering that Alston does not hold a large regular market we feel disqualifies its claim — it does however have much more to offer. Nobody could ever describe Alston as pretty — there is far too much left of its origins as the centre of the local lead mining industry for that. What Alston does have is character and the fact that it is so remote adds much to what has to be described as a unique atmosphere. The cobbled streets are so steep that those not quite so sound in wind and limb have problems, and when you look at the old market cross half way up the main road through the town it is not surprising that an out of control lorry demolished it in 1971. The authorities took their time to replace it but in 1980 they responded well by building a faithful reconstruction. The original was paid for in 1764 by Sir William Stephenson who was a local boy made good and served a spell as Lord Mayor of London.

It is remarkable how the lead mining industry and the Quaker sect are linked and situated on Front Street is a fine Meeting House built in the 17th century but enlarged in 1732, when a lady's gallery was constructed at the rear and this still stands.

The parish church is dedicated to the first Archbishop of Canterbury St Augustine and although there may have been a religious focus here is no certain record of Alston either in the Anglo-Saxon Chronicle or in Domesday. We should not regard this as conclusive, however, since Alston's remote situation may well have prevented documentation. The first written record of Alston church is in 1154 when Henry II appointed Galfrid

The delightful little water mill at Brampton near Dufton.

to be rector, a post he held until 1189. Throughout most of the Middle Ages the area was dominated by the Earl of Derwentwater and the church bell and clock both relate to the family who lived at Dilston Hall. The reason these artefacts reached the church is a sad story because the Earl backed the wrong side during the 1715 rebellion by the Stuarts against the Hanoverians. The Earl lost his head and the family lands were given to the commissioners of Greenwich hospital. In 1767 the commissioners gave the bell and the clock from Dilston Hall to Alston church, the bell having been first cast in 1714 but subsequently re-cast by the church in 1845. It is the clock, however, which is of the greater interest and is thought to be 16th century in origin. It only had one hand to record the hours and in 1978 it was restored and is now kept inside the church as a working exhibit. The present church is not the original which had become so ruinous in 1770 it was demolished, but the work was not well done and in 1869 the present building had to be built and was consecrated in 1870.

From the market cross a number of narrow alleyways lead down towards the South Tyne river, one of these leading to the Butts, an area where the local menfolk practiced their skills in archery which were essential in the days when Alston had to protect itself from the same outlaws who so threatened

Milburn and other border villages. The butts were close to the River Nent, a tributary to the South Tyne. It was illegal not to practice archery from the time of Henry VIII and this was only repealed in 1745. Another alley leads to the High Mill, the wheel of which is being gradually restored by local enthusiasts raising the money. The process is likely to continue through the 1990s. The dark mill enclosing the wheel is freely open throughout the summer but we feel that a nominal sum ought to be charged and the money used to provide some bright lighting, a little information but the balance used to speed up the repairs. Alston's High Mill is important as it is a reflection of the economy of the North Pennines. The first mill was established on this site as early as the 14th century, its power generated by water carried along a mill race which ran through the town. The race provided water for other industries and was also used to wash the streets which are so exposed that grit blown in by the wind has always been a problem. The mill provides grain for an expanding population, and its profits swelled first the coffers of the Derwentwater family and then, as we have seen, those of the Greenwich Hospital for Seamen. Records of the mill began in 1735 and would only be of local interest if it was not for the involvement of John Smeaton who is now best known for his design of the Eddystone lighthouse. It is not often realised that Smeaton's reputation was built upon his ability to design, build and maintain mills. Smeaton designed and rebuilt the High Mill in 1767. He realised that the main problem with the mill was that the water supply along the town leat was limited; he therefore designed a wheel with a large diameter of 30 feet (9.1 metres), but with a very narrow rim. This was only 10 inches (25 cms) and thus made maximum use of the limited water supply. Smeaton's mill continued to work until 1817 when a more normal wheel of 21 feet (6.4 metres) diameter and a 26 inch (90 cms) rim was installed, although the town's other demands upon the supply had probably diminished by then. Much of Smeaton's original design does remain, however, and is being retained by the work of the North Pennines Heritage Trust.

John Smeaton, born in Leeds in 1724, was already a renowned engineer by the time he was in his mid-20s and his work in and around Alston was remarkable. It was Smeaton

The narrow gauge railway running from Alston is enjoyed by walkers and cyclists looking for wonderful scenery while enjoying a rest on the journey.

who was instrumental in bringing the bell and clock from Dilston to the church and he also constructed the Nent Force Level which was much frequented by the Victorians in search of tourist attractions. This was a subterranean drainage tunnel constructed between Alston and the lead mines up on Nenthead. Once the lead mines closed the underground canal left abandoned became a popular tourist attraction and had led to an ambitious project to drive a canal through the Pennines. Whether this would have been attempted if the railway had not arrived is an interesting subject of debate.

The main railway ran between Carlisle and Newcastle with one of the stops being at Haltwhistle, where it was fed by a branch line running up to Alston. Since 1984 part of this narrow gauge railway has been an increasingly popular tourist attraction. Alston's Tourist Information Centre is situated in the old ticket office and there is also an attractive little cafe with some of its tables, protected by colourful umbrellas overflowing onto the platform. On the opposite side of the line is a large free car park and an associated picnic site close to the South Tyne river along which runs a footpath fringed by trees including ash, alder, and willow plus an assortment of spring flowers including lesser celendine, moschatel and coltsfoot. One of the joys of discovering a new area is to search out unusual presents for loved ones at home or to remind oneself of a favourite spot. On sale in the Information Centre are archive and modern photographs of the South Tynedale railway itself but also of the Settle to Carlisle line. What a pity that the old stations of Horton-in-Ribblesdale and Ribblehead could not be converted into Information Centres as good as this one at Alston.

Both line and station were taken over by the South Tynedale Railway Preservation Society following the closure by British Rail in 1976 more than 120 years after it had been constructed by the Newcastle and Carlisle Railway Company. At present the line only runs as far as Gilderdale but there are plans to extend it as far as Slaggyford with a new station built at a half way point. The views from the little train, driven by one of two steam locomotives, are dramatic especially about half a mile from Alston where it crosses the South Tyne on a three arched viaduct. Engine No 6 came from a mining complex in Spain and therefore is ideally suited to run from Alston. It has been named in honour of Thomas Edmondson who invented the old type of cardboard railway ticket. The other engine, Chrzanow came from Poland, and both locomotives are popular with photographers who love the black smoke and white steam gushing from various parts of their anatomy and with the children who see a more tangible connection between a small locomotive and Thomas the Tank Engine, a copy of which most of them seem to buy from the shop. It is possible to buy a joint ticket for the railway trip and for a visit to the Killhope Wheel described in Chapter 10.

It is a pity that the rail-link cannot connect with Haltwhistle which is one important base from which to explore Hadrian's Wall, crossed by the Pennine Way, which runs via the South Tyne Bridge and Park Fell to join the old Roman track called Maiden Way. Much of the route is not clearly defined but there are usually many day-explorers on the Maiden Way which is one of the branches off Ermine Street. Continue on past Slaggyford, Knaresdale, Lambley and Greenhead, at which point crossing the Tipalt Burn into the Northumberland National Park.

However tempting it may be to use Haltwhistle as a base to explore Hadrian's Wall we prefer to use Hexham one of the most vibrant market towns along the whole length of the Pennine Way.

CHAPTER 12

The South Tyne Gap, Hexham and the Roman Wall

North of Alston the Pennine Way continues but actually it is now something of a fraud because technically the Pennines end here and beyond the Tyne Gap give way to the Cheviots. We should therefore call this the Cheviot Way but this could be even more confusing. The Roman route called Maiden Way follows closely the line of the Pennine Way for a distance of 26 miles from Kirkby Thore once in old Westmorland but since 1974 in the new county of Cumbria to Carvoran in Northumberland.

We have a love of Hexham, but it may be that we were influenced by a most delightful summer Tuesday with the market in full swing. Few open air markets are so attractive with flower and vegetable stalls overlooked by an abbey church. The first charter was granted by Henry III in 1239, originally being on a Monday, but in 1662 when Charles II was King the day was changed to Tuesday. Around the market square are other buildings in addition to the abbey and which reflect the history of the town to such an extent that the area has been designated a conservation area. There is a cross of red sandstone, a long market colonnade which provides some shelter for a minority of the traders, and a castle-like moot hall which was built around 1400 and where Archbishops' Courts were once held with its modern use being as an exhibition centre. Through the gate of this tower is the old jail built in 1330 and looking rather like a Florentine palace. These days it has been refurbished and the top floors house the very well laid out Border Museum which is open from Easter to October. There is a fine collection of books and also a wide selection of archive sounds and folk music relating to the area. There is an exhibition of the border wars. On the substantial ground floor is the Information Centre.

Hexham Abbey was founded in Saxon times and the crypt dates from AD 674 and is one of the finest in Britain. It is said that the first church may have contained the bones of St

144

Hexham market is overlooked by the magnificent abbey.

Andrew to whom it was dedicated; the stones almost certainly were taken from the Roman fort at nearby Corstopitum near Corbridge. After a period of rough treatment at the hands of the Danes the abbey was re-established by the Augustinians around 1113 but the building is unusual in that its church was not finally completed until 1908. The choir which is magnificent is 13th century but the roof is two centuries later. The trancepts are also 13th century and on the west wall the old night stairs still stand, well worn by the feet of monks descending from their dormitory to begin their day's devotions. The furnishings of the church are remarkable by any standards and include a large Roman monument to Flavinus who was a standard bearer and he is shown crouched over a Briton who is striking up at his assailant with a dagger. There are a lot more Roman artefacts here and also an Anglo-Saxon cross which was erected in AD 740 at the grave of Bishop Aeca. This church is a photographer's delight but Hexham's custodians do not welcome cameras although there is a fine collection of postcards in the well stocked shop.

Below the abbey are gardens shaded by some of the finest copper beeches we have ever seen plus willows close to a stream overlooked by seats which in May are surrounded by bluebells and other spring flowers. Growing beneath the shade of an ash we discovered a clump of moschatel, its tiny green flowers earning their old name of Town Hall Clock. The petals are arranged like the four faces of a clock with a fifth 'clock' pointing skywards which enabled God to keep an eye on the time. There are also a number of pleasant strolls along the river especially the Tyne Green Riverside Country Park sited close to where the North and South Tyne tributaries join to produce the main river. The area was once a common and given to the town in 1887 by W.B. Beaumont who became the first Lord Allendale, and it is now a real amenity for the town and its increasing number of visitors. For a fee there is windsurfing to the west of the bridge, small boats and canoes are for hire, fishing permits are available and there is what is known as a Trim Track with activities such as parallel bars and other gymnastic apparatus. There is a picnic and barbecue area plus a network of paths along the wooded riverside near the bridge.

From the park is a splendid view of the substantial bridge completed in 1793 after three other spans, including one designed by Smeaton had been washed away at times of flood.

No student of Roman history or indeed the Pennines can afford to miss spending time on and around Hadrian's Wall, which was obviously built across the Tyne Gap. It ran from Bowness-on-Solway in the west to the obviously named Wallsend in the east. Between them are 73 English (80 Roman) miles or in modern terminology 117 kilometres. The best tribute to the choice of site between the Pennines and the Cheviot and to the skill of the builders, is the fact that the Wall still stands. As we found at the Castleton caves one needs to save up the entry fees needed at the main centres and take a couple of days to explore what is on offer. To the Pennine discoverer only the central section of the Wall needs to be studied with Corbridge, Chesters, Vindolanda and Housesteads the main focus of attention. In addition to these major centres the Wall itself should be walked and the milecastles examined with many of these easily accessible and free of charge. The whole Wall has been quite rightly designated as a World Heritage Site. Originally built for defence against the proud and independent Caledonian tribes as well as to serve as the Roman equivalent of a linear custom's post, the engineers intelligently used the contours of the land and followed the upliftings of mainly basalt rock. This provided the best possible visibility to the north where most of the danger was likely to originate, although there was some preparation made for a sneak attack from the rear. It was not just a mere wall, however as there was also a ditch, a vallum and a military road. The ditch was built to protect the northern side of the Wall and its V shape had an average depth of 9 feet (2.75 metres) and a width of 27 feet (8 metres) and was thus a formidable obstacle in its own right. In some areas where stretches of wall have gone, probably taken by generations of farmers for use as building stone, the ditch still exists and has been used to map the route.

The vallum runs more or less parallel to the wall but this time on the south side, and is an even more impressive ditch than that to the north. It is usually about 70 yards (64 metres) from the wall and is around 10 feet (3 metres) deep and 20 feet (6 metres) wide at the top but was less wide at the bottom. The earth dug out during the construction was piled up to create a further obstacle. The entrance across the vallum to the wall was under strict military control and it was also the custom's barrier.

This complicated feat of engineering required efficient communications and there are two excellent roads associated with the wall. The Military Way was built to connect all the forts, milecastles and turrets and was a sturdy stone structure running straight between the Wall and the vallum and being about 20 feet (6 metres) wide. It enabled troops to be moved along the wall out of sight of any belligerents and then they could emerge from the milecastle gate and create a surprise. Just to the south of the vallum ran Stanegate which was the main public road across the north of England. Thus we have five parallel feats of engineering running between the Tyne and the Solway. The concept behind the idea was one miracle, the fact that it was built so quickly was an even greater miracle. In AD 122 Hadrian who later became Emperor of Rome came to troubled Britain and soon appreciated the military difficulties posed by an unprotected border. By AD 125 the wall was being built, supervised by Aulus Platorius Nepos and by AD 135 the structure was largely complete. In the period between AD 190 and 200, the garrison had to be withdrawn to deal with a serious series of revolts in continental Europe. The northern tribes of Britain, never slow to recognise weakness, broke through the wall at several points. Once they had solved their European problems the Romans, under the orders of Emperor Septimus Severus, restored the wall and it remained impregnable until the fall of the Empire in AD 383 and it never functioned again in anger. But what a glorious 250 years the wall enjoyed and how lucky we are that the entry fees to the most attractive areas have been wisely spent on restoring and interpreting one of the world's most important monuments. Those who think the entry fees a little steep would do well to consider how the revenue is being used.

The remains at Corbridge on the Newcastle side of Hexham and just a little way from the Pennine Way should also be visited as the ruins are not merely piles of stones. Here can be seen the walls and floors of the granaries with ventilation ducts running under the stone floors and an aqueduct feeding a stone water fountain, which bears the scratches caused by the Roman soldiers sharpening their swords. The museum and its exhibitions which are open daily is our idea of how such an establishment should be run. The displays are clear, the illustrations colourful yet accurate and the young are catered for and gather eagerly around an animated map which plots the movements of the various legions by the use of flashing lights. Corstopitum as the settlement we now call Corbridge was known in Roman times, was not actually on the wall itself, but it was the nerve centre and the military supply depot removed to the rear and away from the possibility of direct attack. Its setting is truly spectacular with the buildings of brown stone contrasting delightfully with the lush green of the fields.

Chesters is a fine example of the determination of Roman builders to stick rigidly to the architects instructions and there was no way that they would allow the River North Tyne to upset their plans. Rather than deviate around the river they simply built a bridge, and then a fort called Cilunum to protect it. Close to the river are the remains of one of the finest bathhouses to be found in Roman Britain; the walls are up to 10 feet (3 metres) high in some places and within are boiler rooms, warm rooms, cold rooms and other areas required to fulfill what was not only a hygienic function but also an important social amenity at that time. Much talking and even military planning was conducted in the bath house. There is a great more to see around this site which is delightfully maintained. The headquarters building is reached via a flight of steps and overlooks manicured lawns. Inside is an underground storeroom where the money was kept and even more importantly the legions battle standard.

Vindolanda situated at Bardon Mill is not open during December and January and only opens at weekends in November and early February; for the rest of the year it opens daily from 10 am. It lies to the south of the wall and was the frontier home for the soldiers. Excavations have resulted in a welcome insight into the family life of the legionaries. There is even an exhibition of the games played by Roman children. Rare documents have been discovered in which writing was scribed with ink on thin sheets of wood. There is also a pair of locally made leather shoes and a slipper which quite remarkably still bears the maker's name. The 'Cinderella' who owned this slipper was either well travelled, well-to-do or perhaps both since the maker Lucius Aebutius Thales was a well known Roman shoemaker working in Gaul and to import his work cannot have been cheap. The museum in which these, and other artefacts, are displayed, is housed in Chesterholme a 19th-century solid stone house reached from the Vindolanda ruins via a zig-zag path into a deep valley lined with colourful gardens.

Actually Vindolanda is older than the wall itself and was originally on Stanegate built following Gnaeus Agricola's conquest of northern Britain which was substantiated by forts. The civilian settlements which they protected were constructed around AD 85. Vindolanda is set above the South Tyne and recognisable among the ruins including bedrooms, dining room, kitchen, latrines and stables. The Vindolanda Trust have carried out the reconstruction of a section of wall and they have also built a turf wall which was built as a sort of template prior to completion of the western area of the wall.

Housesteads is the most complete Roman fort in Britain and its popularity is best appreciated from the road. The latest of our many visits, was on a Bank Holiday Monday and we found the car park overflowing and crowds of visitors having been filtered through the shop were winding their

way up a steep path to the five acre fort shaped like a
playing card and from which there are the panoramic views
including back to the line of the Pennines and on towards the
Cheviots which would have been so vital to the soldiers. Among
the recognisable buildings are granaries, latrines, a hospital,
commanding officer's accommodation and a barracks which at
peak activity would have been home to as many as 1,000 troops.
Among their duties would have been the security of the border
crossing and custom's post.

The modern road which runs past Housesteads is on the line
of Wade's Road. This was constructed by the military in the
1750s following General Wade's death but resulting from his
experiences during the 1745 rebellion when it was difficult
to move his troops. Now surfaced by modern materials the
undulating road runs straight as an arrow for several miles
along the line of the wall and is thus a popular tourists' route.
Many visitors make a stop at either Once Brewed Visitor's
Centre or at Haltwhistle which has long been popular with
those who base their walking on rail travel. Once Brewed stands
not upon the wall but close to the vallum and here is based an
Information Centre run by the Northumberland National Park.
Whilst the Wall naturally features in the displays it also traces
the history of man in the area since the Ice Ages. The centre
is open from Easter to the end of October.

The Pennine Way passes close to Housesteads and Wade's
Military Road and also near enough to Haltwhistle for many
walkers to use this area as a base from which to travel either
southwards to Alston or northwards to Bellingham.

CHAPTER 13

Haltwhistle to Bellingham and the Tyne Gap

As Haltwhistle is a stop on the railway between Carlisle and Newcastle it is tempting to imagine the name deriving from a halt and a whistle. This flight of fancy is not correct. The original spelling was Hautwessel and some of the local people still pronounce it this way. The name has been in use since 1254 and is Old English meaning a stream by a hill. It lies very close to the Tyne Gap which technically is a low lying area of land between the South Tyne river and the pretty little River Irthing a tributary of the Eden. This marks the northern limit of the Pennines proper the land beyond the gap is the start of the equally beautiful Cheviots.

Haltwhistle with a history of agriculture, coalmining and recently light engineering has a compact Information Centre which is an integral part of a leisure complex including a swimming pool and surrounded by a large car park. In the season this spot attracts tourists like bees to Pennine heather. Clutching their leaflets about Hadrian's Wall most visitors head out of the settlement which some guide books have described as a dull grey market town. This is a pity for the parish church of the Holy Cross is one of the finest in Northumberland and partly dating to the 13th century. From the outside there is nothing remarkable about the building which has no tower, but there is a bellcote. The interior is a joy and a model of spacious design and fascinating furnishings. Much of the early English church remains including a nave with aisles; the chancel, however, does not have any aisles leading off it and its roof line is lower than that of the nave. There are interesting monuments, including the tombstone of John Ridley who died in 1562 and the brother-in-law of the martyr Nicholas Ridley who is mentioned later in this chapter. There is also an effigy of a 14th-century Knight plus three ornately carved coffin lids dating to the same period. The church guide suggests the font dates from 1676, but also points out that the carvings upon it could be of an earlier date. Much restoration was carried out by the Victorians but the Holy Cross seems to have been handled gently and skillfully; the screen, some stained glass probably the work of Morris and a painted chancel roof would persuade even the sternest of critics to accept that the Victorians had a soul.

The church is cradled gently behind the market place from which lead streets containing some historic buildings including the Red Lion which incorporates part of a 14th-century pele tower built as a defence against the Scots. Peles were a feature of the border country and provided a home for the influential families who lived in the upper rooms whilst in times of danger the local people and the animals could seek shelter in the lower rooms. Many of these are now ruinous and some were used by marauding bands of so called moss troopers in the 16th and 17th centuries who preyed like cattle rustlers on the border farms. Some peles, however, are in fine condition including Featherstone Castle which is around three miles outside Haltwhistle on the banks of the South Tyne. The original pele is 14th century but in the more peaceful days of the Jacobean period a fine dwelling house was attached and in the 19th century other extensions were constructed. The hall is not open to the public, but there are fine views of it from river and Featherstone Bridge built between 1775 and 1780 is an attractive span. Another example of pele tower architecture is at Moteswick about 5 miles from Haltwhistle now a farmhouse but once the sturdy home of the one time influential Ridley family. Here Nicholas Ridley was born and he eventually became Bishop of London. He was one of many clergy to fall foul of Mary Tudor who tried so hard to re-establish the Catholic faith following the death of Henry VIII. Many clergy resisted bravely and paid for their faith by being burned at the stake. The grizzly list included Bishop Ridley and his friend Latimer who perished in the flames at Oxford in 1555. Moteswick has not one tower but two and also a 14th-century gatehouse which gives a real impression of strength.

Across the river from Haltwhistle is Bellister, another castle based upon a tower, this time a 16th century structure to which is attached a house built around 1669. Thus the area is not only Roman wall country but a land of Northern English castles. It is a pity not to stay longer but the Pennine walker has to head for the Cheviots. The walk is tough here and follows the line of the Wall and then across country to Wark Forest and Kimmin's Cross to Bellingham close to the banks of the North Tyne and which describes itself as the Capital of North Tynedale. It is also an easy route to follow by road leaving Haltwhistle on the B6318 part of the Military road to Chollerford to Wark-on-Tyne and then via the B6320 to Bellingham. Each of these places is worth exploring in its own right whilst along the route are several handy parking places close to footpaths and super little picnic areas.

Chollerford set astride the North Tyne is yet another honey-pot for tourists as here is another fine memorial to the Romans. At Chesters the wall meets the River North Tyne and a bridge was built which then required a fort to protect the crossing. They called it Cilernum but we now know it as Chesters, after the country house which was built from stones from the Roman fort, which housed cavalry. It is now maintained by English Heritage and the entry fee includes parking, toilets, good facilities for the disabled and in summer refreshments are available. The complex is open daily except December 24–26th. The fort has been extensively and carefully excavated and the museum includes a good collection of sculptures and Roman inscriptions. The fact that there is so much left is due to the work of the one-time owner John Clayton who was born in 1792 and became one of the finest classical scholars of his age. By the time he died in 1890 Clayton had ensured Chesters of fame in the annals of Romano-British history.

Chollerford itself is a historic place close to which stands a wooden cross which marks the site on which Christianity is said to have begun in Northumbria. Here in AD 634 was fought the battle of Heavenfield when the young Christian King Oswald overcame the heathen forces of Cadwallon. Oswald then felt safe enough to invite Aiden and his monks from Iona to preach in Northumbria, which then included much of northern England. Oswald was quite rightly made a Saint and many churches, including that at Chollerford, were dedicated to his memory. Heavenfield is close to Wade's Military road (B6318) which crosses the arched bridge at Chollerford over the North Tyne and from this a signed footpath leads to a Roman bridge. There is a splendid view of the Wall winding its way up to Brunton turret yet another fine reminder of the extent of this ancient monument.

The scenery on the route to Wark-on-Tyne has been dramatically altered by extensive and initially insensitive planting of alien conifers especially spruce. This has softened and smothered what must have been typical scenery and those following the Pennine Way now have to wind in and out of dense forest. If this is a definite negative there are some positive features for those who are prepared to seek them out. Wark Forest Nature Trails have been laid out by the Northumberland National Park authorities and on the banks of Warks Burn, a tributary of the North Tyne, is Stonehaugh Picnic site which in addition to its natural beauty has a collection of decorative totem poles and the feeling of being in Indian country attracts many visitors. Also nearby on Haughton common is the site of Kimmin's Cross (spelt Comyn's cross on the O.S. maps) of which the foundations only are original. Legend has it that Kimmin was a northern chief killed here by the jealous son of King Arthur who had been entertained by the unfortunate man at his castle thought to have been situated at Sewingshields.

Whilst Bellingham claims to be the capital of Upper North Tynedale Wark would seem to have an equally legitimate claim. At the time when the region was firmly under Scottish rule there was a court held here on the site of a Norman motte and bailey castle. Even earlier Wark was the scene of the murder of the Christian King Alfwald of Northumbria in AD 788 an event which held back the advance of the conversion of these parts to the faith. The church at Wark is not remarkable although attractive in appearance but in the churchyard is the grave of Abel Chapman one of the world's great naturalists. His first book called *Bird Life of the Borders* was published in 1889 and around his home at nearby Houxty Chapman listed 134 species of bird. Two points must be made here. Firstly Chapman was also classed as a 'sportsman' which means that he shot the birds he professed to love. Those of us, born in an age of conservation, should remember that at this time the Keartons were developing the technique of bird photography and those then wishing to look closely at the wildlife were obliged to shoot first and then rely on the

St. Cuthbert's church at Bellingham has a stone slabbed roof which resisted attempts by the Scots to fire it.

skills of the taxidermist to produce a permanent record. The optical equipment available in Chapman's day was poor and we who make use of excellent binoculars during our field trips should be aware of this. Secondly the records made in Victorian times were prior to the days of the forestry

The Lang Pack grave at Bellingham is more likely to be based on fact than folklore.

plantations. Abel Chapman travelled the world but was drawn back to his native parts because, it is said, he could not bear to be away from the haunt of the black grouse, his favourite bird. His vast collection of big game trophies are in the Hancock Museum in Newcastle-upon-Tyne and given the apt title of 'Abel's Ark'.

It matters not to us whether Wark or Bellingham is the true capital of North Tynedale — they are both attractive or perhaps historic would be a better word. Bellingham has a market day on Monday and with early closing on Thursday. It lies in an unspoiled area between the Pennines and the Cheviots. It has remained remote because it never lay on a major route and it is this tranquility which now makes it a popular place to take a quiet walking holiday and present accommodation caters for all tastes and budget. Bellingham — its early name and the way it is still pronounced was Belling-jum — is on a bridging point over the North Tyne. Here the De Bellingham family built an earth and timber castle with the permission of the King of Scotland for whom they served as Royal Foresters. Near the railway station is a large grassy mound which is probably the site of the early fortification. Throughout the Middle Ages the border fluctuated with the Scots being a real thorn in the side of the English and this is reflected in the structure of St Cuthbert's church which has an unusual stone-slabbed roof. This was probably built following a series of raids during which the church roof was set on fire. The churchyard has an even more dramatic tale to tell, there being a strange gravestone in the shape of a huge sack. Here is the last resting place of the robber of Bellingham who does seem to have some substance in fact. More than two centuries ago it is said that a pedlar visited Lee Hall on the outskirts of the town and was allowed to leave his pack. A maid saw the bundle move and called another servant who discharged a gun into the pack which then produced a moan and a pool of blood oozed out onto the floor. A plot to burgle the hall had thus been foiled but the pedlar's accomplice was apparently given a Christian burial, with an apt gravestone provided.

Apart from the Pennine Way itself there are a number of fascinating walks based on Bellingham and for which self-guided leaflets are available. Our favourite leads through a wooded area to Hareshaw Linn a 30 foot (9.1 metres) high waterfall near which breed both dipper and grey wagtail. The wooded area offers breeding sites for treecreeper, great spotted woodpecker, sparrowhawk and both starling and house sparrow here using natural niches in hollow trees. Close to the path is the remains of a 19th-century iron-works, and for those who look closely the track of the old

Kielder Water during its construction in the 1970s.

railway which once carried the coal in and the processed iron out.

In the centre of the town is a good Information Centre and within an easy car driving distance is Kielder Water, a huge man made area of forest and reservoir now one of the most popular tourist areas in the North East and organised on the lines of an American National Park. A pleasure craft operates on the water, wind surfing, boating, pony trekking, orienteering and angling are all encouraged and in the winter the area is well known for its excellent bird watching. There are two very impressive Visitor's Centres based upon Kielder Water. At Tower Knowle on Yarrow Moor near Bellingham the National Park and Water Board have combined to produce a comprehensive exhibition of the history and natural history of the area plus audio visual presentations. There is also a cafe, a shop and it is from this point that the passenger ferry operates around the lake. The Kielder Castle Visitor's Centre is based upon a Gothic style shooting box established by the Duke of Northumberland in 1775. There is also a cafe here and a comprehensive exhibition on the setting up and management of the forest

The ferry boat *Osprey* approaching the pier on Kielder Water.

and there are short walks from the centre to a number of observation hides from which a variety of wildlife can be observed. For those who prefer to drive a toll road of around 12 miles leads through the forest to the A68 road at Redesdale.

The Bellingham area thus has a great deal to offer, but there are occasions when special events bring the whole area to life. On the last Monday in May Bellingham holds a fair and there are plenty of sideshows, stalls and novelties whilst the last Saturday in August is show day with craft displays, Cumberland and Westmorland wrestling, working dogs and clay pigeon shooting. The fact that it is still sheep country is reflected in the livestock sales which take place in January, May, August, September and October — this is the time to see and listen to the local accents of the leg-pulling farmers who are not as humourless as they are often said to be.

Among the tangle of new forest and close to the line of the Pennine Way is the village of Byrness one of six such habitations constructed in the 1950s to house forestry workers and designed by Thomas Sharp. Some of the houses are now empty, but two have been converted into an attractive youth hostel and another is now an Information Centre. There is also a petrol station and a cafe within the village. The little 18th century church of Old Byrness contains an interesting stained glass window, which is a memorial to those who died during the construction of Cateleugh reservoir which was completed in the 1870s and supplies Newcastle some 40 miles away with around 10 million gallons (45 million litres) of water each day. It has a capacity of 2,305 million gallons (10,478 million litres). The church window is 'in memorial to those men, women and children who have died during the construction of the reservoir at Cateleugh.' Some idea of the equipment used in the construction industry of those can be appreciated by studying the window which depicts steam engines, wheel barrows, picks and shovels, saws, axes, and a child sitting on the ground with his father's dinner wrapped in a handkerchief. The reservoir was so large that it took over a thousand men more than fifteen years to complete. Byrness is thus interesting in its own right, but can also be regarded as a good base from which Pennine Way walkers can launch their final assault on the route. It is also one possible gateway to the Cheviots, but the market town of Wooler is by far the largest and most popular place to use as a base.

CHAPTER 14

Wooler to Kirk Yetholm via the Cheviot

Being a border town Wooler was frequently burned and in consequence few old buildings remain the majority dating to Victorian times. Despite this, however, the attractive market town has an atmosphere which many a more architecturally undisturbed settlement would be proud of. There is an Information Centre in the town which is usually open during the summer and there are many leaflets and books available describing the district and the Cheviots and the fertile Milfield basin which it shelters. The air is fresh here and it is reported that the lighthouse keeper's heroine daughter Grace Darling came to Wooler in an effort to cure her consumption. Alas this failed to work the wonder and she died.

The Cheviots form a natural barrier between England and Scotland and this ensured that Wooler was much frequented by the border reivers as the rustlers of sheep and cattle were called in these parts. Actually there are two breeds of sheep found in the region, the hardy blackface which roams the upland and the relatively less tough Cheviot which is the breed favoured in the valley areas. An even hardier sheep can apparently be produced by crossing Cheviot rams with blackface ewes. Some crossing has also been done using Leicesters. The Cheviot is typified by being hornless, white faced, short woolled and especially because of its neck region which resembles an Elizabethan ruff. In contrast the blackface which earns its name is a horned breed. Our old friend Eric Halsall, famous for his television programmes 'One Man and His Dog', has taught us to respect sheep and the shepherds and their families who live in these remote places and give their lives to their flock. Many upland cottages still echo to the rhythmic clicking of the spinning wheel which gives them something to do during the long nights of winter.

The highest point of the Cheviot is 2,676 feet (816 metres) above sea level and it is a long extinct volcano, but capped these days by a very soggy peat bog and grassed over in the drier areas which is, as we have seen, ideal for sheep. It is probably that the volcano was active around 380 million years ago and the granite core and andesite lavas have been weathered to produce cone shaped hills with smooth tops created mainly by the action of ice. Outcropping is quite rare in this region but there are some, the most impressive being at Henhole which is so shaded that snow often lies in its shelter well into June. Other fascinating names are applied to areas of metamorphosed lava including Long Crags, Langlee Crags, Auchope Cairn and the Hanging Stone. This is named after a packman's load had slipped over the edge and the strap tightened round his neck and strangled him. Around the foothills above Wooler the conclusion of the Ice Ages produced meltwater channels which are now dry valleys and at Monday Cleugh and Powburn these can be clearly seen.

As one would expect this area has seen its share of bloody battles with two being of particular ferocity — at Homildon Hill and Flodden. The Homildon Hill conflict took place in 1402, and the English were victorious against the Scots, the conflict being about 1½ miles to the west of Wooler close to the present A697. This was nothing to the carnage of Flodden field near Branxton also close to the A697. It was fought on the 9 September 1513. The first time we visited Flodden was actually on September 9 1972 and the gentle late summer evening gave a haunting feel to the battle field. Being north country folk living on the Lancashire-Yorkshire border it seems that almost every influential local family in these parts during the early 15th century sent troops to Flodden. In the battle 5,000 English were killed but they still defeated the Scots who lost nine thousand men and their King, James IV. A cross erected only in the early 20th century records the event and reads 'Flodden 1513, To the brave of both nations.' Such carnage was bound to echo down the centuries, no doubt aided by the Scots lament 'The Flowers of the Forest' but mainly because of Sir Walter Scott's novel *Marmion.*

Scott also tells the tale of *Black Adam of Cheviot* one of the most evil of the Borderland bandits and the '*Minstrelsy of the Scottish border*' records the grizzly details. The bandit burst in on a wedding party when Wight Fletcher the bridegroom had gone to fetch the priest, but before he returned Black Adam had relieved the guests of their valuables and first ravished and

The church at Kirk Yetholm.

then killed the bride. Fletcher tracked the evil man to the Hen Hole but Black Adam escaped by leaping a 21 foot (6.4 metres) gap into a cave in the side of the cliff. Hen hole may have its evil tale to tell but its reputation is high in the annals of botany because here grows the green spleenwort and parsley fern plus both the star and mossy saxifrage, dwarf cornel and the alpine sowthistle.

For those who are reasonably sound in wind and limb it is a good idea to follow the Pennine Way over the Scottish border and down into Kirk Yetholm which stands at the end of the path. It is, however, perfectly easy to reach the village by car and this attractively haunting little spot should on no account be missed. Actually there are two settlements here — Town Yetholm and the much older Kirk Yetholm separated by a pleasant little stream called Mowmont Water. Although the present church is relatively modern the churchyard is of interest because here are buried many of the Scots who were killed at Flodden. Yetholm was for centuries the gypsy capital of Scotland and it was here that the Romanies crowned their queens. Walter Scott knew the area well and used one of these Queens named Jean Gordon in his character *Meg Merrilees*, the unfortunate lady coming to an untimely death as a witch on a ducking stool in Carlisle in 1745. The last of the Queens named Ester Faa Blythe died at Kirk Yetholm in 1835. There is a row of cottages opposite the Border hotel and overlooking the village green still called Gipsy Row and Gipsy Palace is a nearby tiny cottage with a porch draped with ivy. Perhaps Kirk Yetholm became a gypsy stronghold when Queen Elizabeth banned them from England in 1563 and many may have crossed the border for safety. Not all gypsies travel purely by horse and caravan, many once walked looking for small jobs or working on pots and pans which they sold and earned their name of tinkers. Some think that the word tinker should be tinkler and is an onomatopoeic word sounding like the impact of a hammer on a light anvil.

Whilst the Pennine Way ends at Kirk Yetholm and there is some accommodation available in the area, those contemplating following the route in the reverse direction may prefer to stay at Kelso which is in our opinion one of the finest market towns in Scotland. On our last visit to Kelso, January rain swept down

The Border Hotel at Kirk Yetholm — the end of the Pennine Way.

from a leaden sky and water ran along the cracks between the cobbles of the streets being driven along the gulleys by a strengthening wind. Despite this the town square, its wide expanse open to the elements remained as elegant as on a warm day in June and the Cross Keys an 18th-century coaching inn was doing a roaring trade. Kelso Abbey, although now a ruin is a delight and although not in England, where Henry VIII was dissolving all monastic institutions, it still suffered from his policies.

Between 1544 and 1545 Henry ordered the Earl of Hertford to ensure that the borderlands of Scotland were 'tormented and occupied as much as they can be' and as a result of his orders some 300 buildings were destroyed, Kelso's lovely abbey included. In July on a warm moist morning we once watched a pair of swallows feeding their young in a nest on a ledge of one of the walls of the ruined church.

Thus we have ended our Pennine Journey during which we found the blend of history, natural history, geology and geography, literature and legend to be irresistible. At the beginning we both accepted the popular view that it is best to follow the Pennines from south to north. As we checked the proofs of this book we also followed the route in the opposite direction and found that it made no difference. As stated in our introduction we never had any intention of following the long distance Pennine Way footpath in one continual walk — this is beyond our physical abilities, but then there are many books about for those who are able to enjoy this exercise. What we have done in the production of this book is to explore most of the route and the surrounding areas on foot and by car. At the end of our efforts we are conscious of how much more the Pennines have to offer.

Further Reading

Banks, F. R. (1950) *Guide to the Cheviot Hills* (Reid)
Binns, A. P. (1966) *Walking the Pennine Way* (Gerrard)
Brown, A. J. (1931) *Moorland Tramping in West Yorkshire* (Country Life and Newnes)
Brown, A. J. (1949) *Striding through Yorkshire* (Country Life)
Bruce, C. (1957) *Handbook of the Roman Wall* (Read)
Collins, H. C. (1950) *The Roof of Lancashire* (Dent)
Collins, Herbert C. (1974) *South Pennine Park* (Dalesman)
Cooper, Edmund (1973) *A History of Swaledale* (Dalesman)
Edwards, K. C. (1962) *The Peak District* (Collins)
Emett Charlie and Hutton Mike (1982) *Walking Through Northern England* (David & Charles)
Freethy, Ron (1988) *Exploring the River Aire* (Countryside)
Freethy, Ron (1988) *Northern Abbeys* (Countryside)
Hardy, G. (1985) *North to South along the Pennine Way* (Warne)
Hillery, C. (1990) *Northumberland National Park* (Discovery Press)
Lousley, J. F. (1950) *Wild Flowers of Chalk and Limestone* (Collins)
Marriott, M. (1968) *The Shell Book of the Pennine Way* (Queen Anne Press)
Miller, T. G. (1981) *Long Distance Paths of England and Wales* (David and Charles)
Oldham, K. (1960) *The Pennine Way* (Dalesman)
Palmer, W. T. (1951) *Wanderings in the Pennines* (Skeffington)
Peel, J. H. B. (1969) *Along the Pennine Way* (Pan)
Pilton, B. (1986) *One Man and his Bog* (Corgi)
Porter, J. (1980) *The Making of the Central Pennines* (Moorland)
Poucher, W. A. (1966) *Peak and Pennines* (Constable)
Raistrick, A. (1968) *The Pennine Dales* (Eyre and Spottiswode)
Rowland, M. A. (1991) *Short Guide to the Roman Wall* (Butler)
Savage, E. M. (1974) *Stoodley Pike* (Todmorden Antiquarian Society)
Slack, Margaret (1984) *Portrait of West Yorkshire* (Robert Hale)
Thorold, Henry (1980) *County Durham — a Shell Guide* (Faber)
Wainwright, A. (1986) *A Pennine Journey* (Michael Joseph)
Wood, B. (1971) *Yorkshire Villages* (Hale)
Wright, C. J. (1987) *A Guide to the Pennine Way* (Constable)

Index